"In a world marked by busyness and burnout, *Mindful Silence* offers us both an exit strategy and an invitation. Phileena Heuertz has written a must-read for anyone desiring to live a more mindful, meaningful life. Read this book and learn from one of the great spiritual guides of our time."

Jonathan Merritt, author of *Learning to Speak God from Scratch*, contributing writer for the *Atlantic*

"In reading Phileena's wonderful book on mindful silence, I am reminded of Thomas Merton's words: 'To allow oneself to be carried away by a multitude of conflicting concerns, to surrender to too many demands, to commit oneself to too many projects, to want to help everyone in everything is to succumb to violence.' We live in a society where we celebrate the violence of too much work, media, music, food, drink, and merriment. Phileena's insights sound the clarion call for the church to offer less, not more, and to offer contemplation instead of altercation. Phileena has given us a practical resource to cultivate healthy, mature faith. I'm thankful for her presence and voice found in these pages."

Gideon Tsang, pastor, Vox Veniae, Austin, Texas

"In a world full of noise and a Western church that often replicates the distractions, Phileena Heuertz gives us a road map for finding our way back to spiritual roots and practices that reorient ourselves and our communities. Phileena weaves history, personal reflections, and instruction as she invites readers into intentional silence to create space for us to engage with God and ourselves."

Kathy Khang, activist, author of *Raise Your Voice*

"I can't think of a single person who wouldn't be helped by Phileena Heuertz's *Mindful Silence*. But people like me—who write, speak, and preach for a living—will find special gifts here because the deepest currents of awakening and discovery only begin to flow in us through the intentional, practiced silence of the contemplative way."

Brian D. McLaren, author of *The Great Spiritual Migration*

"What a treat! In these pages, meet people who knew God well and discover what helped them do that!"

Jan Johnson, author of *Meeting God in Scripture* and *Abundant Simplicity*

"In this modern world our attention is being demanded, pulled in every direction. 'Sleepwalking,' as Phileena so eloquently defines it, is a way of life. In our culture, our sense of wonder of the natural world has been replaced by technological advancements, solitary contemplation by social media, and discernment by distractions. To break out of these habitual patterns takes self-realization and the deep desire to take a step back from this monotonous life and focus on actually living it. This is not an ambiguous feel-good self-help book to find God, but it suggests practical, real, hands-on ways in which we can encounter our Maker. From contemplative and centering prayer, to practices of solitude and implementing the Enneagram, this book will entice you to be more than a reader but also a doer of its words. If life 'to the full' (John 10:10) is what you desire in your own journey, then this book will serve as the ideal road map to your destination."

Stephen Christian, vocalist for Anberlin, worship pastor at Calvary Albuquerque

"Phileena's thoughtful words and practices are like water and sunlight for the soul. As I strive to find mindful silence in my own life, this gift of a book will be my trusted guide."

Ryan O'Neal, producer of Sleeping at Last

"Phileena has provided an extraordinary service to Christians today who desire to become more deeply aware and spiritually mature in their daily walk. By providing the history and context of daily meditation and prayer practice cultivated in the first two thousand years of Christianity, she has filled a vast gap linking practicing the presence of the living God to this great lineage. She then makes this very practice come alive in its eternal power—'yesterday, today, and forever.' Furthermore, Phileena very generously reveals her vulnerabilities and discoveries of the power of daily mindful contemplation within her own life. She walks the talk, and in so doing she provides a vision for how we might encounter a profound deepening within our lives too. This is a vital and necessary book, and one that I will keep beside me in my daily practice from now on."

Bobette Buster, professor of storytelling, Northeastern University, Boston, author of *Do Story: How to Tell Your Story so the World Listens*

"Phileena's *Mindful Silence* is a beautiful field guide for sustainable social action through contemplation. A timely book that offers practical tools and powerful insights for a generation grasping for methods of self-care."

George Mekhail, executive director, Church Clarity

"This book is a wheel and a well: it moves us from a deeply human space to a refreshingly divine hope. For a book whose title involves silence, its contents evoke resonance and high volumes of sweet vibrations. I am better because of this important work."

Marlon Hall, lecturing anthropologist, author of *Unearthing You*

"Phileena Heuertz brings together the wisdom of Christian mystics past and present with her own sage vision of contemplative spirituality. *Mindful Silence* penetrates the heart and mind, pointing us to return to the wellspring of life found in the still small voice that emerges when we engage solitude, silence, and stillness long enough to hear it. Phileena reminds us that to do justice in Jesus' name, we must actually be still. She taps into her own experiences on the frontlines of religious nonprofits to illustrate how our zeal for justice for the oppressed must be tethered to a contemplative spiritual practice, rooted in the life that is truly life, Jesus himself. *Mindful Silence* is sure to become a classic of our time."

Larycia Hawkins, Woodrow Wilson Department of Politics, University of Virginia

"With an honest disarming style, Phileena Heuretz names a multidimensional tragedy of our times: fragmentation, hurry, and alienation from our Source. In *Mindful Silence*, this wise teacher of contemplative arts guides us toward healing and reunion with love's ultimate ground, which imparts peace and courage like nothing else can."

Amos Smith, author of *Be Still and Listen*

MINDFUL
SILENCE

THE HEART
OF CHRISTIAN
CONTEMPLATION

PHILEENA HEUERTZ

Foreword by Richard Rohr
Afterword by Kirsten Powers

IVP Books

An imprint of InterVarsity Press
Downers Grove, Illinois

InterVarsity Press
P.O. Box 1400, Downers Grove, IL 60515-1426
ivpress.com
email@ivpress.com

InterVarsity Press® is the book-publishing division of InterVarsity Christian Fellowship/USA®, a
movement of students and faculty active on campus at hundreds of universities, colleges, and schools of
nursing in the United States of America, and a member movement of the International Fellowship of
Evangelical Students. For information about local and regional activities, visit intervarsity.org.

All Scripture quotations, unless otherwise indicated, are taken from the Inclusive Bible, The First Egalitarian
Translation™ Copyright © 2007 by Priests for Equality. All rights reserved.

While any stories in this book are true, some names and identifying information may have been changed to
protect the privacy of individuals.

Labyrinth image on page 115 provided courtesy of Kathy Mansfield.

Cover design and artwork: David Fassett
Interior design: Daniel van Loon

ISBN 978-0-8308-4649-8 (print)
ISBN 978-0-8308-7223-7 (digital)

Printed in the United States of America ∞

InterVarsity Press is committed to ecological stewardship and to the conservation of natural resources
in all our operations. This book was printed using sustainably sourced paper.

Library of Congress Cataloging-in-Publication Data

Names: Heuertz, Phileena, 1973- author.
Title: Mindful silence : the heart of Christian contemplation / Phileena
  Heuertz ; foreword by Richard Rohr ; afterword by Kirsten Powers.
Description: Downers Grove : InterVarsity Press, 2018. | Includes
  bibliographical references.
Identifiers: LCCN 2018028336 (print) | LCCN 2018034259 (ebook) | ISBN
  9780830872237 (eBook) | ISBN 9780830846498 (hardcover : alk. paper)
Subjects: LCSH: Contemplation. | Silence—Religious aspects—Christianity. |
  Mindfulness (Psychology)
Classification: LCC BV5091.C7 (ebook) | LCC BV5091.C7 H479 2018 (print) | DDC
  248.3/4—dc23
LC record available at https://lccn.loc.gov/2018028336

P   25   24   23   22   21   20   19   18   17   16   15   14   13   12   11   10   9   8   7   6   5   4   3   2   1

Y   37   36   35   34   33   32   31   30   29   28   27   26   25   24   23   22   21   20   19   18

For my parents

whose unwavering love and support

has carried me to the heart of God

time and time again.

CONTENTS

FOREWORD

Richard Rohr, OFM

WHAT AN HONOR to offer this foreword to Phileena's fine new book. *Mindful Silence* is an excellent example of how quickly and clearly *the transmission*—and that is what it is—of contemplative teaching is occurring in our time. These pages well illustrate how even younger people are rediscovering the older Christian tradition in ways that both continue the past wisdom and even add to it—because of the access we now have to global sources, travel, and other disciplines that previous times did not enjoy.

All I can presume is that God is becoming very impatient to spread the contemplative mind into our suffering and divided world. The process of transmission seems to be clearly accelerating while also broadening and deepening. What took centuries to clarify now comes to us with new conviction, precisely because we know that these are not *new* teachings, these are not just *our* thoughts or teachings; but we can now know by much easier access to universal sources that we are building on the Perennial Tradition that has been taught, lost, found, and refound again and again, both in the East and in the West.

And this is another finding! Phileena writes here with such simple clarity—and easy readability—because she knows she does not need to prove, convict, or defend anything. *Mindful Silence* contains not just her wisdom but the spiritual wisdom of the ages that is again standing the test of time and showing itself in the fruits of *incarnational holiness.* It is the Great Tradition of action and contemplation again showing itself.

G. K. Chesterton, the English writer and lay theologian, believed that "tradition is democracy extended through time." He goes on to say that "I cannot even separate the two ideas of democracy and tradition. It seems to me they are the same idea." And wouldn't it make supreme sense that God would make access to God completely democratic and available? How could holiness possibly be understood or practiced only by scholars, monks, recluses, celibates, or formal theologians?

As Evagrius Ponticus, that early Syrian deacon, put it, "If you pray truly, you are a theologian, and if you are a true theologian, you will pray." *It always comes back to the authenticity of this inner dialogue that we call prayer.* Then we are all theologians in the way that matters and heals.

Without such inner hearing, and at least tentative responding, I suspect we are all merely the apostle Paul's "gong booming or cymbal clashing" (1 Corinthians 13:1). Without Martin Buber's inspired guidance about the possibility of an actual "I-Thou" relationship, most religion and even spirituality remains "a lesson memorized, a mere human commandment" as both Isaiah says (29:13) and Jesus quotes (Matthew 15:8). This is what so much of the world is now—rightly—rejecting. It is a time of perhaps necessary iconoclasm and rebellion.

But this is not what Phileena is offering you here! Instead she places us back into the Great Conduit that has always been flowing for those who will allow the Flow. As Jesus says "on the last and greatest day of the festival . . . 'If any person is thirsty, let them come to me, let them come and drink'" (John 7:37). We hope it is not yet the last day of the divine festival, despite the immense suffering of our times, but here you are being offered a very satisfying drink from "the fountain of living water" (7:38) that never ceases to flow—and not in spite of the suffering of our times—but in some very real ways, precisely because of it.

Phileena's wisdom, so well represented in the pages of this excellent book as well as integrated in her work at Gravity, a Center for Contemplative Activism, could not have become so clear and so compelling if she and her cohorts were not also in deep caring about the immense suffering of our time—planetary, political, human, animal, and elemental. This holistic response is the unique way of Jesus and his followers, no matter what their formal religion. Nothing smaller will work anymore.

CHAPTER ONE

SLEEPWALKING

So let's not be asleep, as others
are—let's be awake and sober!

1 THESSALONIANS 5:6

Silence is God's first language; everything
else is a poor translation.

THOMAS KEATING

MY DOG, BASIL, is the most wonderful dog I've ever known. Tender, attentive, and compliant, Basil always wants to be together. Though we both cherish our walks along the lake and playtime in the park, we don't have to be doing anything to enjoy simply being in one another's company. Being in silence together is rather easy for us; except on those occasions when Basil has had enough of sitting around and I on the other hand want to meditate.

There's been more than one time when I've been in contemplation, attempting to let go of each and every thought passing through my stream of consciousness, and Basil has sat directly in front of me and nudged my hand or my knee. I'm well-schooled in contemplative prayer, so I know the rules: "As soon as you get caught up in a distraction, let it go, and return to your breath or sacred word." So, I'll notice Basil staring at me and trying to get my attention, but I'll let it go and return to my meditation practice. Then it's a battle of wills. Basil can be very determined, eventually using his voice with a muffled growl to communicate that he wants to go outside.

Contemplative practice is simple but it's not easy—especially when your fur baby wants your attention. But it's even more difficult to stay connected to our soul in daily life, amid a myriad of competing demands, needs, and responsibilities. Staying connected to our true self is all the more challenging when others confront us with anger, aggression, or manipulation.

But it's when life delivers pain and suffering that our soul is really exposed. Sometimes our experiences betray our beliefs. We might believe that God is good, but if God is good, why is there suffering? Perhaps you've found yourself wondering, if God is good, why did my partner cheat, my child die, or my parent endure an agonizing death?

Life has a way of dumfounding our religious paradigms.

Moreover, though Christians profess to follow Jesus and his teachings, rarely are any of us able to live up to his standards. For example, it's one thing to *believe* we should love our enemies and forgive seventy times seven, but try putting that into practice when you have been victimized or when your enemy is a mentor, a clergy member, or a friend you once trusted.

Orthodoxy and religious beliefs are fine until life circumstances betray them. Actually, the central question for our life of faith revolves around *orthopraxy*: How do we *practice* what we believe, especially when life gets stressful, difficult, and painful?

Contemplative spirituality, Christian or otherwise, helps us embody our beliefs and values, especially when life gets challenging. Contemplative practice helps us cope with life.

One very popular expression of contemplative spirituality is mindfulness. Everywhere we turn these days, it seems, this meditation practice has gained traction. Rooted in Buddhism but packaged as secular, mindfulness is the practice of paying attention to what is arising in the present moment. By practicing mindfulness, we deepen our awareness and perception. But it doesn't require faith to engage in it. People of various professions and religions practice it.

Medical science has demonstrated remarkable physical benefits of a contemplative practice like mindfulness. Evidence reports it helps improve disorders such as depression and anxiety; lower blood pressure, cholesterol, and blood sugar; reduce inflammation, infections, and pain; and overcome chemical addictions such as smoking and alcoholism. It has been linked to better sex, and it may even slow brain aging. You may have come across the popular program Mindfulness-Based Stress Reduction (MBSR) at your medical or wellness clinic, public school, local gym, or at the company for which you work. For decades now, Western society has experienced the scientifically confirmed benefits of Eastern meditation.

Buddhism is not the only spiritual tradition to offer such a practice. In Hinduism, we find transcendental meditation. Islam offers dhikr. And Christianity provides contemplation. All great religions have a contemplative stream—an undercurrent of wisdom and spiritual practice that helps us transcend our biologically hard-wired central nervous system's fight, flight, or freeze response to stress. God knows we could all benefit from a practice that helps us manage life better.

Mindfulness is attractive to people in the West because we value reducing stress and feeling better. But these are byproducts of a much more revolutionary project found in the contemplative tradition—the deconstruction of the self. Contemplative practices were designed to awaken us to truth, not to cure illness.

Contemplative spirituality is a way of seeing. The English word *contemplation* comes from the Latin *contemplatio,* which means to look at, to gaze attentively, to mark out a space for observation. Contemplative practices are those that create margin to pay attention to and observe our life. This assumes we have determined to take responsibility for ourselves. It involves some introspection—not for the sake of inner knowledge, but for the sake of living a more skillful life. With self-awareness comes greater understanding of our pain and the way we cause suffering. Contemplative prayer offers an antidote. Through contemplation we find alleviation of our personal suffering, and we discover how to minimize our infliction of suffering on others. Over time, as we engage in contemplative practice, we become less self-absorbed and able to be of greater service to others.

This requires effort and patience. So, we take up a contemplative practice to make regular time for this critical observation of reality. Contemplative practices are held by postures of solitude, silence, and stillness. In solitude, we develop the capacity to be present. In silence, we cultivate the ability to listen. And in stillness we acquire the skill of restraint or self-control.

Christian mystics have always held that silence is God's first language. It's unfortunate we are not more acquainted with this language. Silence is consciousness itself, the Source of all that is. The heart of Christian contemplation beats with silence and expands our consciousness.

> THE HEART OF CHRISTIAN CONTEMPLATION BEATS WITH SILENCE AND EXPANDS OUR CONSCIOUSNESS.

Life happens. It's out of our control. What *is* in our control is how we respond. A commitment to contemplation is an agreement to take responsibility for our actions and relationships. Religious teaching tries to awaken us to such accountability.

One of my favorite spiritual teachers, and personal mentor, is a wise Cistercian (Trappist) monk named Father Thomas Keating (hereafter referred to as Father Thomas). He introduced me to the Christian contemplative tradition many years ago, and my life has never been the same. I'll never forget how he said, "If you stay on the spiritual journey long enough, the practices that sustained your faith will fall short. When this happens, it can be very disillusioning. But if we stay on the journey, we find out that this is actually an invitation to go deeper with God."

That's what happened to me.

WAKING UP

When I landed in West Africa's Freetown, Sierra Leone, it was suffocatingly hot. Sixty percent of the country was still controlled by the rebel forces, but the ten-year war over blood diamonds was slowly coming to an end. Soldiers were being disarmed and brought into UN peacekeeping camps.[1]

Refugees from all over the country were pouring into the capital city—survivors of brutal mutilation and children displaced from their parents. Both the government and rebel forces used amputation as a tactic for fear and control of the population.

There seemed to be no mercy for this horrific demonstration of war. Young and old people alike were subjected to having one or both arms chopped off. In some cases, sons were forced to commit the grotesque act on their parents.

The only consideration given was the audacious choice between "short" or "long sleeve"—indicating where the severance would take place on the arm.

These brave and broken people struggled with basic daily chores like washing, dressing, and embracing loved ones. Many of the men, farmers, needed *both* hands to work the land. They faced the despair of not knowing how they would ever provide for their families again. Needless to say, my early life in middle America did not prepare me for this degree of human suffering.

As if meeting the adult survivors of this brutality wasn't enough, I encountered children who had also suffered under the wicked knife of their oppressors. One child was only three months old when the soldiers brutalized her. We met her when she was two, struggling to open the shell of a peanut using her one hand pressed against the nub that was left of her other little arm.

While at the camp for the war wounded (essentially a slum community for thousands of survivors of mutilations), we were introduced to a number of teenage girls who wanted to share their story with us, hoping the world would then know what had happened to them. They were desperate for someone, anyone, to do something to respond to their unbearable circumstances. So, I bolstered up the courage to listen and bear witness to their pain.

I heard detailed accounts of how the soldiers came to their village and rounded up the people. I heard how the combatants sexually assaulted and systematically amputated the limbs of their mothers and murdered their fathers. I heard how they then assaulted the young girls, often gang raping them repeatedly, and forced them to be their "war bride," which meant they would be subjected to domestic and sexual slavery.

As the girls recounted the sordid details through glassed-over eyes, some of them held their babies—children conceived from the sexual violence they'd suffered.

I left the camp in a daze. I couldn't believe the horror my new friends had survived. Before that day, I thought I'd seen it all.

For many years, I had helped establish communities of justice and hope all over the world among impoverished children with HIV and AIDS, destitute youth living on the streets, and survivors of sex trafficking. But I had seen nothing that compared to this kind of inhuman cruelty and anguish.

Immediately I looked for someone to blame: the government and warlords whose greed led to such human atrocity. Certainly, there were systemic structures of injustice at play that were to blame—much like the systems of global economic disparity with which I had grown familiar.

But as I recalled the stories of the soldiers who brutalized these young girls, I found particular human faces who were responsible and should pay for their crimes. Anger and judgment stirred in me toward the soldiers who had committed such unspeakable brutality.

And then I visited the camp for young soldiers who had just recently been disarmed. Boys of all ages, and as young as five or six, gathered together to meet with us. That's right—children involuntarily enlisted to fight as soldiers. And like the young girls, they too wanted to tell their story.

In moments, a few teenagers were directed to us. How could I bear to sit down with the soldiers who were responsible for the horrific suffering of the girls I'd met just the day before?

Somehow, I did.

And the boys began to recount similar stories of militant invasions of their village, the murder of their parents, and being conscripted into war. They remembered being drugged and forced to cut off arms and legs and to take up weapons that were too heavy for them to carry. They remembered being given girls to violate as the war dragged on.

It was all too much for me to bear. Combatants. Just children. Forced to grow up under the parental authority of warlords. As I listened to my little brothers, to the suffering they'd endured and the guilt they lived with, and as I remembered the agony of my younger sisters, I was struggling once again to find someone to blame. The soldiers I had so easily judged and convicted the day before were now sitting in front of me with a sea of pain in *their* eyes. It was now not so easy to demonize them.

It's a natural human tendency to look for a scapegoat—someone to blame for suffering and injustice. In the Hebrew Scriptures, we learn about the scapegoat as the innocent animal used in religious ritual during Yom Kippur. All the sins of the people were symbolically placed on a lamb, which was then released into the wilderness as a way of cleansing the people of their imperfections and wrongdoings (Leviticus 16:8-10). This, in a sense, gave them a clean slate to start anew. A short historical study reveals that Greeks and Romans had similar practices, using a goat, a dog, or even women and men as an instrument of atonement and cleansing. This resulted in communities casting out, stoning, and sacrificing those deemed unacceptable. Scapegoating is an example of the myth of redemptive violence, common across many cultures and in many Christians' understanding of the crucifixion of Jesus—believing Jesus was the symbolic "goat"

needed to placate God. Father Richard Rohr, Franciscan priest, my
trusted spiritual teacher and personal mentor (hereafter referred to as
Father Richard), has helpful teaching on this:

> Humans have always struggled to deal with fear and evil by ways
> other than forgiveness, most often through sacrificial systems. . . .
>   If your ego is still in charge, you will find a "disposable" person
> or group on which to project your problems.

> *Jesus became the scapegoat to reveal the universal lie of scapegoating.*
> Note that John the Baptist said, "Behold the Lamb of God,
> who takes away the *sin* [singular] of the world" (John 1:29).
> It seems "the sin of the world" is ignorant hatred, fear, and
> legitimated violence.
>   *Jesus became the sinned-against one to reveal the hidden nature
> of scapegoating* and so that we would see how wrong people in
> authority can be—even religious important people (see John
> 16:8-11 and Romans 8:3).[2]

And so there I was in Freetown surrounded by mass agony, attempting to apply redemptive violence by looking for someone to blame,
stone, cast into the wilderness, or crucify. As my heart tore open, I
wondered, *Who is responsible for all this suffering?* And not only *this*
suffering, but who is responsible for *all* the pain in the world? I wanted
someone to blame.

But I couldn't find the culprit. As I traced the lineage of oppressor
and victim, it seemed everyone had been victimized. I had run out of
people to project my judgment onto, so I subconsciously directed my
anger toward God. I wondered, *If people are basically victims victim-
izing one another, and God created us, then surely God must answer for
this. God must be to blame.* I thought, *Perhaps God is not all that good
after all.*

Have you ever felt that way? In the face of despair have you doubted
God's goodness? What blows has life delivered you? An illness perhaps? Or an unwanted divorce? Suffering is suffering, so don't

compare yours to someone else's. Instead, consider events that have taken place either in your life or in the life of someone you love. Has it been a struggle to accept those circumstances?

Those many years ago, facing the trauma of a nation torn apart by war, I found myself plunged into a crisis of faith. What I had learned about God growing up in the Protestant pews of Indiana was radically challenged in the face of human need. My worship had dried up. I had no words to pray. Scripture no longer inspired me. And God seemed painfully silent.

I was afraid. I didn't know how to engage such silence. I thought something must be wrong with me. I felt as if I didn't have enough faith; or even worse, something must be terribly wrong with God.

Thankfully, Father Thomas came into my life right on time.

Early one spring Saturday morning, my husband's spiritual director left a voicemail inviting the two of us to have dinner with his beloved teacher, an elderly monk that we'd never heard of named Thomas Keating. We were mesmerized at dinner by this tall, humble, Gandalf-like figure dressed in a black robe. Turns out, his religious order, the Cistercians, observe a strict rule of silence. It was out of his deep well of silence that his life radiated so much peace and wisdom. Following dinner, Father Thomas gave a teaching and closed with a guided centering prayer practice.

Father Thomas's teaching was like a wellspring to my arid soul. With gentle authority—the kind of credibility that comes from experience—he opened a portal to God's nourishing presence. He helped me realize that I didn't need to be troubled or discouraged by God's *felt* absence and grueling silence. Like an old transistor radio, I just needed to learn how to tune in to this new frequency. After that day, I found courage to give myself to the silence with all of its darkness, questions, doubts, and pain. And it was there, in the great, deafening silence, that I woke up.

The allures, distractions, and pace of our time, coupled with our inner illusions of self, others, and God, threaten to keep us asleep and at bay from the Source of our existence, purpose, and rest. Most of us go through life sleepwalking. It's not easy to wake up. Usually it takes a crisis of some sort to do so: an unexpected career transition, a feared medical diagnosis, a miscarriage, a natural catastrophe. But contemplative prayer aids the waking process too.

In the face of agony in Sierra Leone, my faith fell short. Forgiveness for such horrific wrongs seemed like an impossibility. Healing for my friends and their nation seemed completely out of reach.

When I had a hit a wall and come to the end of myself, contemplative prayer, in the form of a Christian meditation method called centering prayer, became the only way in which I could attempt to encounter God. There, in solitude, silence, and stillness, I could just show up—as I am with all my doubts, questions, and pain. And over time, the gentle, secret, grace-filled presence of God began to reveal a love so enormous that it has the power to transform all the pain of the world—beginning with my own.

DYING

Little did I know that waking up was going to be followed by the invitation to die. Perhaps if I had known that, I would have resisted or refused to awaken. Of course, I'm not talking about a physical death, but rather a *spiritual* death. Waking up was followed by an invitation to let go of who I thought I was. Remember, the contemplative tradition has one main objective: the deconstruction of the self.

So, if you're curious about where the contemplative path leads, I'll cut to the chase: death. Death to your short-sighted self-will. Death to your self-serving ego. Death to your limited sense of self.

This may come in the form of a dramatic culmination or in many small deaths over time. Death is one of the seven stages in our pilgrimage of soul, but it's not the final stage. Along the way there are usually a series of many minor deaths. These small deaths support the other stages that I outline in *Pilgrimage of a Soul: Contemplative Spirituality for the Active Life*.[3] The other phases—awakening, longing, darkness, transformation, intimacy, and union—are preludes to death and at the same time the fruit of dying. Like a labyrinth, we cycle in and out of these stages in the journey home to our true self.

Contemplative spirituality is an invitation to wake up and die so you can truly live. Contemplative prayer is for courageous, devoted seekers. It facilitates personal transformation for a world in need of healing love. Contemplative spirituality supports the way of following Jesus, which necessitates dying to self or emptying self to make room for the all-consuming presence of God (Philippians 2). But we are reluctant to choose this road less travelled. It's easier to walk through life asleep.

Sleepwalking takes the form of deeply embedded unconscious illusions about self, God, and others. These distortions orient us toward psychological, behavioral, and spiritual attachments, compulsions, and addictions, which over time lead to general unhappiness. This is what Christian tradition calls imperfection, sickness, or sin.

> CONTEMPLATIVE SPIRITUALITY IS AN INVITATION TO WAKE UP AND DIE SO YOU CAN TRULY LIVE.

Our addictions may not take the form of chemical cravings (though it can turn into that) but at the core reside in our compulsions to be identified with what we have, what we do, and what others say about us.[4] We are enslaved to our unconscious impulses and do everything we can to satiate our inner discontent: nonstop scrolling through social media, which only magnifies our unhappiness; unnecessary shopping in the hopes that more stuff will make us feel better; overeating or drinking to drown and dull the inner ache. We have any number of escape routes from pain, but the path of transformation is learning how to be *with* the pain so new life can emerge in and through us. Contemplative spirituality teaches us how to do that.

Trying to satisfy our desire for power and control, affection and esteem, and security and survival, we grow more and more dissatisfied with our self, God, and others. Father Thomas refers to these desires as "programs for happiness." He says that these three programs for happiness emerge from very basic biological needs. It is a natural part of our human development to seek a degree of power and control, affection and esteem, and security and survival. The problem is that, in time, we over identify with one by way of compensating for that basic need which may have gone largely unmet in our childhood. Then our *need* turns into an unconscious *compulsion*. We crave its gratification, unable to be happy or content when life fails to deliver the amount of power, affection, or security we desire. Our personality forms around this attachment. An overly emotional reaction to life exposes our vulnerable condition.

Have you ever reacted emotionally to a situation or a relationship and later wondered why you responded so strongly? As we grow in self-awareness, we often realize that some of our reactions to present circumstances are actually in response to past events that are buried in our unconscious. The current situation provides a trigger for the unresolved pain. When we recognize the agony surfacing, we are experiencing grace. This is an invitation to greater healing and wholeness. Contemplative spirituality helps us wake up to this dynamic at play in our unconscious.[5]

At a young age, we fell asleep to our interior anguish. That sense of being utterly alone, separated from others, and unlovable was too painful to acknowledge. In order to cope, we unconsciously built up fortifications to protect this most vulnerable self. In essence, this formed our personality.

Personality comes from the Greek word *persona*, which means "mask." Our personality is not our true self. But because we think it's too risky to expose our inner pain, we create a mask and we hide. We think our mask, our personality, will be more lovable. But you can see the dilemma. Our mask enslaves us, keeps us in hiding. We are not free. Instead we grow increasingly alienated over time from authentic connection with others. A tragedy for sure, given we all want to belong.

In our attempts to self-protect and be happy, we end up yearning for that which cannot ultimately satisfy. Sure, it might dull the inner ache briefly. Compulsive scrolling through social media might momentarily help us feel less lonely, for example. But once the digital stupor wears off, our inner unconscious misery begs again to be filled. It's like drinking a glass of saltwater when you're thirsty. At first it satiates, but then it leaves you sick. Eventually we learn what kind of nourishment really satisfies. The cycle of torment and emptiness continues until, by grace, we awaken (become conscious) to the inner void.

After my visit to Sierra Leone jolted me awake, I found myself in a season of inner excavation. The surface layer of pain—associated with the victimization of young boys forced to become vicious soldiers and young girls enslaved as domestic and sexual servants—uncovered secondary pain. I had come up short with answers and solutions to such desperate human need, which revealed the next layer of my aching heart. Layer upon layer of self-awareness ultimately revealed a wound in my psyche. The shape of my wound? A young girl who didn't know she was loved just as she is. I soon came to realize that I had constructed my life in such a way that I wouldn't have to face that primordial pain.

Now, the shape of *your* wound may be different, corresponding to a different program for happiness: a young boy who doesn't feel safe, or a young girl plagued with the fear of having no control. My pain related to the need for affection and esteem. So, at a young age I unconsciously found a way to dull the misery. I found a coping mechanism. If I could just be and do for others, maybe they would find me worth loving. And so, my life unfolded in large part around my compulsion for approval. I made decisions and lived in such a way that others would think and speak well of me. Thus, I would achieve a degree of affection and esteem. Waking up was devastating, because it forced me to come face-to-face with the pain of feeling unloved.

When we become an astute observer and do our inner work, we can identify the shape of the wound that traps us in a cycle of suffering.

The more self-aware we are, the more liberated we become so that, when life wounds us and we experience pain, the suffering has less power over us; it dominates our consciousness less. I like how Father Thomas puts it: we know we're making progress in the spiritual journey when the things that used to drive us up the wall now drive us only halfway up the wall.

In fact, becoming wise spiritual pilgrims allows us to hold our pain, rather than our pain holding and trapping us. Yes, life is painful, but it's also the source of so much joy. And you can't have the joy without the pain. It's the experience of pain that forms our inner well to contain joy. Contemplative spirituality gives us the tools to both embrace our pain and dig our well.

Initially, contemplative spirituality helps us stop sleepwalking. And once awakened, we learn to die to the lies we've lived for so long that keep us in a cycle of unrelenting suffering. Those lies manufactured an entire sense of self, our identity—and it's that self, the false self, that has to die so the true self can be resurrected from its sleep.

For me, this meant dying to the lie that I am who others need me to be. Once I awakened to the realization that I identified with this lie, over time, through contemplation and by grace, I was able to die to that identity. From the dying, a freer Phileena emerged, one who is less controlled by the approval of others. I am now able to be truer to my voice, my needs, my desires, and my dreams, regardless of what others think about me. And in the space of that freedom, I'm able to be of greater service to those around me.

⌐ Who are *you*? What external forces shape *your* identity? In what ways do you feel trapped inside a self that's not the truest you? When you observe your life, what do you see and hear? ⌐

DEAF, BLIND, AND CLOSED-MINDED

Jesus is well known for his ability to heal people who were blind and deaf. Time and again in the Gospels, it is the person pushed to the margins of society, well acquainted with their sense of separateness and sickness, who seeks out Jesus. With desperate openness and receptivity, those most in touch with their need for healing experience remarkable liberation.

And yet, it is often those who possess the sense of sight and sound who are unable to see and hear what Jesus was trying to reveal. "Don't you see or understand yet? Are your minds closed? Have you 'eyes that don't see, ears that don't hear'?" (Mark 8:17-18).

In another seething rebuke from Jesus—if we have an open mind, eyes to see, and ears to hear—we realize he is speaking to many of us today. "Woe to you, religious scholars and Pharisees, you shut the doors of heaven's kingdom in people's faces, neither entering yourselves, nor allowing others to enter who want to" (Matthew 23:13).

Like many good-hearted religious people of Jesus' day, we too often fail to get the good news that Jesus is trying to communicate—essentially, that we are loved, safe, and have no need to fear. We settle for our own poorly crafted heaven, placating our programs for happiness, rather than enter God's liberating kingdom where we live into our inheritance as divine children. To our further shame, in our unawakened state we prevent others from entering the kingdom of heaven who want to. We often miss the mark. And one interpretation of sin is just that—missing the mark.

Contemplative spirituality helps us distinguish between our false and true self. It helps us access real freedom and power to *not* miss the mark. Through contemplative prayer, we learn how to penetrate the center and live into our divine nature (2 Peter 1:4).

A RICH TRADITION

Christian contemplative spirituality is not new; it's simply a new way of seeing in every age. It is, in essence, putting on the mind of Christ (1 Corinthians 2:16; Philippians 2:5-11). Christianity holds a rich contemplative tradition, beginning with the model given in the suffering, death, and resurrection of Jesus. This is the way to abundant life. We can't avoid suffering and death if we want to experience resurrection.

As Christianity developed, contemplation was normalized by the second century with the stress on *contemplatio*, or resting in God for prayer. We see clear expression of the tradition in the writings of the desert mothers and fathers of the third and fourth centuries. These desert ascetics were radical Christians who rejected the corruption of their religion by the Roman Empire. With the emperor Constantine's conversion to the faith, Christianity was no longer a faith on the margins of society, but instead became enmeshed with the empire itself. The church began to lose its prophetic voice to the state. It blended with an empirical agenda for domination and exploitation, which led to all kinds of evil in the name of Christ.

The desert mothers and fathers rejected this distortion of the faith and dared to live a different way of austere solitude, silence, and stillness. They fled to the deserts of Egypt, Palestine, Syria, and Arabia to live lives of prayer, fasting, labor, and poverty. They believed that spiritual practice was essential to enlightenment or union with God. They were determined to keep themselves open and receptive to the transformational work of grace in their life rather than give in to the allures and deceptions of a powerful state that co-opted Christianity. Their spiritual practices formed the foundation of monasticism.

For a few hundred years, the contemplative tradition (also referred to as the wisdom tradition) was simply the way in which Christianity was expressed among the faithful; we didn't need a name for it. But in time, that way would largely get squeezed out of the Christian religion—at least the Christianity of the West. It's unfortunate that the wisdom tradition was mostly lost to modern Western Christianity.

In 1054, Christianity experienced the Great Schism—that canyon-like divide between the Greek East and the Latin West, what became the Eastern Orthodox Church and the Roman Catholic Church. The growing community of early desert mothers and fathers were largely part of the Eastern church. Consequently, the evolving Western Catholic Church viewed the contemplative tradition as more Eastern and distanced itself from something it deemed foreign to its own contextualization.

Already a step removed from their contemplative roots, Protestants were even further detached from this crucial dimension of spiritual formation. By the time of the Protestant Reformation, advocates for legitimate change in the Western church often threw out the baby with the bathwater, abandoning altogether the contemplative tradition of the faith. Protestants therefore distanced themselves further from their contemplative roots than Catholics.

Following the Reformation, we entered the Enlightenment period, or the Age of Reason, with its emphasis on rationalism. This era drove the nails in the proverbial coffin of any contemplative tradition that included nonconceptual prayer practices.

Nevertheless, while the contemplative tradition was pushed further and further to the margins, Christians always maintained a remnant of its wisdom. Throughout these pages, we'll explore a few of the greatest teachers of this vestige and the insight they've left for us.

PRACTICING FAITH

If religion refers to the doctrine and rituals that affirm belief, spirituality is *the way we live our beliefs*. In first-century Palestine, Jesus brought Jewish religious tradition under scrutiny in order to purify it and demonstrate how to embody and practice liberation and transformation. If we have an open mind, eyes to see, and ears to hear, Jesus is scrutinizing the practice of our faith today.

Contemplative spirituality, then, is quite simply a way to *practice faith*. Practicing faith means we clear space within us to encounter divine love so that we might be freed and changed. A truly liberated and transformed person naturally liberates and transforms the world.

So, exactly *how* does one take this narrow road of practicing faith? Through contemplative prayer. Christianity offers several different prayer practices to assist us. While there are few Scripture references that give a specific, prescriptive way to pray, the Bible provides an expansive scope of prayer. It offers examples of many different kinds of prayer, such as praise, petition, lament, intercession, and withdrawal to solitary places.

The overarching theme in Christian Scripture points to prayer as a means of *communion with* God, which leads to personal and collective change. Contemplative prayer is a powerful means to that end. It opens us to a new way of seeing and being in the world.

INTEGRATING CONTEMPLATION AND ACTION

After twenty years leading an international nonprofit that cares for the most vulnerable of the world's poor, my husband, Chris, and I noticed a few unfortunate things about good-hearted Christians trying to build a better world:

1. We're often some of the grumpiest people—carrying the weight of the world on our shoulders.

2. We tend to take better care of others than we do of ourselves.

3. Many of us perpetually teeter on the edge of burnout.

Many of us, not just social justice activists, can relate to this. Sleep-walking through life often leads to grumpiness, self-neglect, burnout, and disillusionment with our faith.

Such short-lived attempts to make the world a better place won't do. The world's need requires our stamina and resilience. So, in 2012, Chris and I set out to "do good" better. We started Gravity, a Center for Contemplative Activism, to ground social engagement in contemplative spirituality. Gravity is for people who care about their spirituality and want to make the world a better place. Our organization exists to nurture the integral connection between mysticism and activism, or contemplation and action. Gravity grounds social engagement in contemplative spirituality by offering retreats, spiritual direction, and Enneagram workshops and consultations.

We give three different kinds of retreats. The Grounding Retreat is a basic introduction for people who want to learn more about the contemplative tradition and prayer practices. The Deepening Retreat is for those who want to develop their contemplative practice. And the Enlightening Retreat is for people who have been on the contemplative path for a while and desire further teaching and guidance.

We offer the service of spiritual direction for people who desire ongoing support for their spiritual journey. Spiritual direction is an ancient practice that dates back to the early desert mothers and fathers and their communities. It's a relationship of spiritual counsel whereby the director supports clients in observing their life and allowing themselves to be observed by God. This gentle yet at times piercing practice helps the client to discern God's presence and action in their life, which always leads to greater freedom to live into their true self.

Working with the Enneagram is incredibly helpful for spiritual development. Gravity's Enneagram workshops and consultations are a crucial part of expanding consciousness. The Enneagram is a sacred map that helps identify your unconscious and subconscious motivations. Circling around nine principal types of human nature, your Enneagram number reveals your path of transformation as well as your path of disintegration. While the Enneagram reveals your personality, it is different from other personality profiles in that it links to your childhood wound. Your childhood wound illuminates your path of liberation. The Enneagram is a powerful resource for the contemplative path, for as it deconstructs the false self, it simultaneously reveals your true self. It helps us offer the best of ourselves to a world in need.[6]

No matter your vocation, whether you're a humanitarian, activist, pastor, bartender, doctor, lawyer, or stay-at-home parent, contemplative spirituality is for you. It helps you live into your best self.

We can "do good" better (which is a confession that we won't always "do good" great) when our active lives are rooted in contemplative spirituality. Contemplative prayer dismantles our unconscious compulsions (for power, affection, and security) and allows the Spirit to flow more freely through us to help heal our loved ones and community.

Contemplative prayer is a gateway to encountering real, transforming love. Sure, there are still problems in the world and in my own life, but contemplative prayer helps me access the love of God in the midst of those difficulties and opens me to ongoing growth. Transformation leads to engaging the world in joy-filled, creative ways. There's no room to be grumpy or fussy when one accesses the divine love that penetrates our humanity and is present even (and most especially) in the most horrific of circumstances.

Contemplative prayer and social action must go hand in hand for effective social change. Otherwise our social action will too often end up being our imperfect will imposed on the world. It's too easy to unconsciously project our own wounds or ego-driven desires onto other people and projects. Contemplative prayer exposes and unhinges our unconscious motivations. One who is committed to contemplative prayer has awakened to their need for healing from these inner wounds and their need for liberation from unconscious compulsions. Waking up makes us much less toxic as we engage others and seek to offer some good in the world.

Jesus said the greatest commandment is to love God and love our neighbor as ourselves. If we put all our effort into taking care of others to the neglect of self-care, then we're disobeying the Great Commandment and headed for dysfunctional relationships—with God, with others, with our work. Social change is possible when we love others *as* we love our self. Contemplative prayer practice is a commitment to love our self so we can love others well. When we allow ourselves to be loved through contemplative prayer, we remember that our identity as the beloved is an identity that we share with all God's children. Eventually, we come to the realization that loving our neighbor as our self means that we are one with our neighbor. To love our neighbor is to love our self, and to love our self is to love our neighbor.

But many of us struggle to accept love.

A commitment to contemplative prayer is a commitment to authenticity—being real with the fact that we ourselves are in need.

Each of us is in need of love, in need of transformation. We don't have all the answers. And sometimes our greatest intentions inadvertently cause harm.

We delude ourselves if we think we hold the answers to the world's problems. If we're honest, we have trouble tending to *our own* personal, relational, community, and national problems. Tending to our personal story of healing and wholeness must go in step with our desire to see the world made whole. Through activism we confront toxicity in our world; through contemplation we confront it in ourselves. The two go hand in hand. This is contemplative activism. It grounds us in divine love and allows us to be a channel of that love.

When we're grounded in love we are less likely to burn out, because love is directing our action, rather than unconscious, distorted motivations. Love's ever-burning flame fuels our life with passion. An effective response to social, economic, and political injustice originates from within a soul who is awakened to her need and is committed to being transformed by divine love. As we are changed through contemplation, the world around us is changed.

> THROUGH ACTIVISM WE CONFRONT TOXICITY IN OUR WORLD; THROUGH CONTEMPLATION WE CONFRONT IT IN OURSELVES.

Contemplative prayer practice effectively keeps us humble and honest. Humility and honesty are essential to building a just world. The more of us who commit to such practice, the more peaceful our world will be.

SPIRITUAL PRACTICE

It's one thing to read about contemplative spirituality, it's another to grasp it. Many of the writings of historical Christian contemplatives and mystics seem obscure and mysterious. It can be difficult to understand the experiences of God they try to communicate. Often, we fear what we don't understand. As we've seen, mysticism and the whole contemplative dimension of the gospel really got sidelined through the centuries. Nonetheless, mystics are simply those who grapple with the Great Mystery—our infinite God who transcends our finite understanding yet makes the Godself known to us. Through the writings of the mystics, we come to learn that practices of contemplative prayer help us begin to engage the Great Mystery.

Practice is another word for discipline. And the English word *discipline* is derived from three Latin words: *discipulus* meaning student; *discere* meaning learn, hear, get to know; and *disciplina* meaning instruction. The single most distinguishing mark of contemplative prayer is discipline—becoming a student who hears and applies instructions. And in a society that is accustomed to instantaneous gratification—even in our prayer life—instituting and nurturing spiritual discipline will not be easy.

It might be more attractive to us if we think of *discipline* in its Latin root intention: spending regular time in contemplative prayer is a way to assume the role of student, be instructed, and get to know God and oneself.

Prayer disciplines exercise our ability to hear and see and to be molded as a teacher forms a student or a potter shapes the clay. If we long for a more meaningful life, one that is transformed by faith—authentic, abundant, and effective—we must adopt practices that reflect that desire and commitment.

Contemplative prayer invites us to empty ourselves of our attachments, compulsions, and addictions so that God can have more space to live more fully within and through us (Philippians 2). This is the way of the Paschal Mystery—the pattern of salvation as seen in the life of Jesus.

Paschal is derived from the Greek word *pascha*, which in turn is derived from the Aramaic and Hebrew term for "the passing over." This evokes memories of Jewish salvation history, when God spared the lives of the Hebrew people. "Mystery" refers to the aspects of Christian faith that cannot be understood by reason and intellect alone. It follows that the Paschal Mystery points to the mysterious ways of the Divine that we are invited into by faith.

Contemplative prayer helps us embody such faith. As we let go of control and yield to God in contemplative prayer, we undergo the way of Jesus—suffering, death, and ultimately resurrected life. The natural order in all of life is death and rebirth. If we want to live the abundant life, we will gladly yield to this process. For the way of the cross is our ultimate peace and fulfillment.

Contemplative prayer addresses our attachment to pleasant emotional experiences—in prayer and daily life. We do not come to contemplative prayer to experience something pleasant but rather to learn how to be content in all circumstances (Philippians 4:12).

So, come with me as we explore these touchstones of contemplative spirituality:

- Withdrawing to Engage
- Finding Liberation by Discernment
- Discovering Darkness Is Light
- Exploring a Deep Well
- Dying for Life
- Unknowing to Know

Let these dynamic cairns open your mind, your eyes, and your ears as you pilgrimage further down the path of awakening, transformation, and wholeness. You'll be guided and supported not only by me but by these prominent wisdom teachers within the Christian tradition: Thomas Merton, Ignatius of Loyola, John of the Cross, Clare of Assisi, Mother Teresa, and the fourteenth-century anonymous author of *The Cloud of Unknowing*.

You'll find a contemplative practice at the close of each chapter to ensure your exploration is not solely an intellectual exercise. Instead, let your reading be a catalyst for interior prayer and growth. Let me encourage you to engage in each of the practices at the end of the chapters: breath prayer, the prayer of examen, lectio divina, labyrinth, the welcoming prayer, and centering prayer.

What these prayers all have in common is a certain degree of solitude, silence, and stillness—practices that are desperately needed in our crowded, noisy, busy lives. It's the degree of solitude, silence, and stillness that sets contemplative prayer apart from other forms of prayer that are heavily reliant on words. Contemplative prayer isn't meant to subvert prayer with words; instead, contemplative prayer complements other forms of prayer.

Each of these modes of prayer helps us assume a passive and receptive posture of mind, body, and spirit, which in turn helps us yield to the presence of God and God's work of radical change in us.

If these practices are new for you, I hope you'll adopt at least one of them in your daily life. And if you already have a daily contemplative practice, by all means, please continue your discipline while you deepen your knowledge of the contemplative tradition.

Contemplation helps us let go of what we can see with the eyes and step into what we can perceive with the heart (2 Corinthians 5:7). Contemplative prayer loosens our grip on attachments, compulsions, and addictions that keep us closed-minded, spiritually blind, and deaf to the inner voice of love. The more we grow quiet and still, the more open and receptive we become to God's action in our soul and, consequently, in our life.

Prepare now to awaken.

Practice: Be Still

This simple prayer helps us begin to grow acquainted with the posture of letting go that is required in all contemplative practice. I learned this prayer of being from Father Richard. The text comes from Psalm 46:10: "Be still, and know that I am God."

To begin, find a quiet place, gently close your eyes, and take a few deep breaths.

Prepare to pray the psalm in five consecutively diminishing sentences.

Either aloud or quietly to yourself, say the words, "Be still, and know that I am God."

Then take a couple deep breaths and pause between each of the following phrases:

"Be still, and know that I am."

"Be still and know."

"Be still."

"Be."

When you feel ready to move on, pray, "Amen."

This prayer can also be prayed with a group. The facilitator leads with each sentence and the group repeats aloud after each consecutively diminishing phrase. The pause between each phrase can be lengthened depending on your need or the needs of the group.

Be still, and know that I am God.

Be still, and know that I am.

Be still and know.

Be still.

Be.

For more information visit gravitycenter.com/practice /be-still.

CHAPTER TWO

WITHDRAWING TO ENGAGE

*Rising early the next morning, Jesus went off
to a lonely place in the desert and prayed there.*

MARK 1:35

*It is in deep solitude and silence that
I find the gentleness with which
I can truly love my brother and sister.*

THOMAS MERTON

SOLITUDE CAN BE a frightening proposition, unless you're an introvert.

However, being alone and entering interior solitude are not the same. We can be alone and still be dominated by our attachments to power, affection, and security. If you're an extrovert you may be quick to assume contemplative prayer is not for you, given its solitary nature. But this couldn't be further from the truth. Just because something doesn't come naturally, doesn't mean it's not for you. In fact, most things that are good for us *don't* come easily.

For example, we know it's good for the body to get exercise. But how many of us really look forward to going to the gym? Though if we neglect our physical health, we know there will be concerning consequences. The same can be said for neglecting our spirituality. Refusing to make time for the spiritual practice of solitude, as well as silence and stillness, can actually lead to violence. The modern contemplative leader and central teacher for this chapter, Thomas Merton, made this point better than anyone.

> There is a pervasive form of contemporary violence to which the idealist most easily succumbs: activism and overwork. The rush and pressure of modern life are a form, perhaps the most common form, of its innate violence. To allow oneself to be carried away by a multitude of conflicting concerns, to surrender to too many demands, to commit oneself to too many projects, to want to help everyone in everything, is to succumb to violence. The frenzy of our activism neutralizes our work for peace. It destroys our own inner capacity for peace. It destroys the fruitfulness of our own work, because it kills the root of inner wisdom which makes work fruitful.[1]

Contemplative practice is the remedy for our frenzied sickness.

Not only is contemplation a cure, but it's the way of the future. In 1982, Jesuit theologian Karl Rahner stated emphatically, "The Christian of the future will be a mystic or s/he will not exist at all."[2]

The historical record indicates that at its birth Christianity most certainly had a mystical core. But by the seventeenth century, the mystical dimension of the Western expression of the faith was relegated to deserts and monasteries. As time progressed, it became more and more difficult for even monasteries to hold on to the contemplative tradition. Prominence was given to the rational mind. So, most Christians in the West today have received a spiritual formation that is dominated by the left brain—the discursive, conceptual, analytical, and judging mind that sees in parts. The religion has, for all intents and purposes, divorced itself from the right brain—the contemplative, non-conceptual, intuitive mind that sees in wholes.

Now, thirty-five years after Rahner's prophetic statement, these two minds of the faith are coming together. It certainly appears we are in the midst of an evolution of human consciousness. More and more

Christians desire to adopt a spiritual practice that exercises the right brain. Many are experiencing the physical, emotional, and spiritual benefits of contemplative prayer. Christianity is no longer in severe opposition to science. Thus, the faith tradition now widely recognizes neurological, medical, and psychological data that reveal the power of meditation to establish an inner state of peace and to aid physical and emotional healing. Furthermore, even prominent mainstream Christians teach that meditation supports one's relationship with Christ. Slowly, people of faith are making the connection between interior spiritual practice (meditation) and exterior spiritual practice (forgiveness, loving-kindness, mercy, justice, and reconciliation).

In fact, we may be in the midst of a revolutionary tipping point—at least in the West. But it hasn't always been that way.

Until recently, with the exception of the mendicant religious orders (like the Franciscans and Dominicans), contemplation and action were basically severed from one another, just like the dissociated minds of the faith. Nevertheless, as early as the thirteenth century, one of the principal teachers of the church, Thomas Aquinas, highlighted three vocational options: the contemplative, the active, *and* the mixed life. Unfortunately, Christian religion essentially limited the choices to two: the active *or* the contemplative.[3] It would take another seven hundred years for the mixed life to become a viable option. The average spiritual seeker today is looking for this very expression of faith and action.

Historically, to be a contemplative meant to take religious vows and be cloistered in a monastery as a nun or monk. The focus for the contemplative life was intended to be love of God and a life devoted to prayer. To be a person of action meant to be of service in society as a diocesan priest or layperson—which incidentally cut one off from the vocation of contemplation. The focus for the active life was love of neighbor and works of mercy.

Aquinas wrote at length about the supremacy of the contemplative life, and the church readily took his perspective. Therefore, because only the few seemed called to cloistered life, contemplation came to be understood as something rare and available to only the chosen few. Contemplation and mystical prayer were seen as highly spiritual, somewhat odd, and cloaked in mystery.

Once the Reformation took place, Protestant Christians for the most part grew ever more distant from the contemplative vocation. By modern times, few lay and even clerical Protestants knew anything about the contemplative dimension of the faith.

In the Christian West, it wasn't until the spiritual awakening of the 1960s that the contemplative tradition began to be renewed for our time.

BECOMING A MYSTIC

The intensity of a vocation among impoverished people led me into a crisis of faith. Coming to the end of our self will often do that. Essentially, I had come to the limits of an active life dissociated from contemplation.

When I started to experience the psychological and energetic benefits of centering prayer, my vocation took on new expression. I didn't serve in the same way that I had before—from my limited false self. I was beginning to serve from what Rahner so eloquently described as "a genuine experience of God emerging from the very heart of existence."[4]

I was awakening to a new dimension of faith—where my beliefs in God were no longer simply intellectual ideals, but rather a lived reality. I was experiencing God in prayer, and I was being changed. Those changes necessarily affected my relationships, my community, and my vocation.[5]

Now, because our ideas of mysticism have been reduced to the ecstatic experiences of saints like Teresa of Àvila (who is known to have experienced trance states and levitation), let me be clear. *My* experiences of God were much, much less dramatic. During centering prayer, there were seldom tangible signs of anything taking place.

Sometimes I would experience intense pain in my back or uncontrollable sorrow evidenced by a waterfall of tears. But most of the time, all appeared quiet and still to the casual passerby.

Sure, my mind might not have been as quiet and still as I would have liked, but slowly an interior silence and stillness was building, which allowed for what Father Thomas calls "divine therapy" to take place. Emotional wounds of a lifetime that I had stored in my body and psyche began to heal. My over-attachment to power and control, affection and esteem, and security and survival began to loosen. My false self came into view. As I learned to self-observe, I was empowered to self-correct.[6] The consequence is being able to live more often from my true self.

As time went on, I was so convinced that contemplative practice was crucial for our community that I wanted everyone to adopt a practice like centering prayer. But few were interested. I remember the push back and resistance: "That way of prayer is for introverts." "I pray by doing." "I experience God in the active life, and that's good enough for me." "Contemplation is for the religious, cloistered life." "That's just navel-gazing."

Even *our* community was affected by the active-contemplative dichotomy of religious consciousness. But I had stumbled into the "mixed life," and like Rahner, I knew it was the way of the future. Our society, our human family, our planet depends on it.

In time, by withdrawing a few times a day for contemplative prayer, I realized that solitude was not a *disconnection from* the rest of the world but instead a necessary recalibration for more meaningful *connection with* the world.

TRUSTING WITHDRAWAL

Recently, after my routine morning meditation and prayer, I was lounging in my chair, reading a well-worn paperback on spirituality, when all of a sudden, my neck and upper back kinked up. I couldn't look up, and I was in severe pain. A visit with a chiropractor later that week revealed through various tests and x-rays that my spine was in grave distress. This had obviously been developing for many years. And when the chiropractor heard about my life and work, he wasn't surprised about the toll it had taken on my body.

I remember when I first realized what a heavy burden I was carrying. In the late 1990s, before I had ever heard of contemplation, I found myself taking a silent retreat at the Abbey of Gethsemani in Trappist, Kentucky. Nestled in the rolling bluegrass hills lies one of the most breathtaking Trappist monasteries in the world. This was once the home of twentieth-century modern mystic Thomas Merton. Leaders from all over the world were known to have visited him there.

By this time, I had been thoroughly baptized in human suffering: the masses of women, men, and children dying for lack of adequate food in India, the multitudes of children living on the streets in Romania, and abandoned widows begging in Nepal.

In response, the humanitarian organization I was a part of had established a couple of children's homes in India for HIV-affected children. We were, quite literally, personally responsible for their vulnerable lives. But this was only the beginning. There was so much more work to be done to address the needs we had encountered around the world.

To assume administrative oversight of the organization, Chris and I had relocated to the tiny, insulated town of Wilmore, Kentucky. Consequently, I was struggling with my newfound circumstances. I had expected to be living in India, serving alongside people in dire poverty. I had spent a few years preparing my heart, mind, and soul for such a calling. I was not prepared, however, to live in the little, rural, Mayberry-like town of Wilmore. It seemed I couldn't get more withdrawn from a world in need.

In Wilmore, I was surrounded by mostly white, middle-class academics and seminarians, single people looking for a spouse, and married couples who were getting pregnant and having babies. I was encircled by people grasping for the American dream. But I had different aspirations. I wanted to do something relevant for the anguished women, men, and children who had burrowed their way into my heart. And then I came to know of this gorgeous monastery, cloaked in silence, just a short drive from my home.

I didn't think I could get anymore withdrawn from the needs of the world than I already was in that little country town. But as I drove out of Wilmore toward the abbey, I did indeed get more and more removed from society. With each mile, I descended deeper into spacious solitude, silence, and stillness. Surrounded by luscious green grass, towering trees, and expansive blue skies, my heart began to open up.

I felt safe.

I felt seen.

I felt free.

As my heart unfastened, I realized I was hurting. I was carrying the weight of the world on my shoulders. And in the grand spaciousness I heard, "My yoke is easy, and my burden is light" (Matthew 11:30).

How could that be? The state of the world and the horrible conditions people were living in felt like a very heavy burden. I wanted a better way to live—where the yoke *is* easy and the burden light.

As my time at the sobering Neo-Gothic monastery progressed, I found myself captivated by these curious men, cloaked in white cowls, who spoke only when necessary. There seemed to be a spiritual lightness and easiness in that place, a different way of being and moving in the world—and I longed to live that way.

After that first visit, I was compelled to go back as often as I could. During those personal retreats, when I could get alone, quiet, and still, I learned how *to be*.

THE GROUND OF BEING

Learning how to be is usually the hardest lesson to learn. And yet it's the foundation for everything we do. Without an established being, our doing is often frantic and frenetic, heavy and burdensome, and bears little fruit. Sometimes it leads us to violence cloaked in good intentions. Sure, we might be "successful" in our doing, but success is different from impact and transformation. Are our accomplishments actually building a better world?

Withdrawing from activity exposes our superficiality and disconnect from the *ground of being*,[7] from our divine Creator. If God is the source of all being, and therefore the ground of everything, how are we to convey any aspect of the divine in our active life when we are so uprooted from the very ground of reality itself? It became clear to me over time that we must *withdraw to engage* if our interaction with the world is to bear any fruit that lasts (John 15:16).

Up to that point, the spiritual formation I had received was rooted in the discursive, conceptual, analytical, judging mind, and prescribed certain beliefs and behavioral standards. But my experience challenged some of those beliefs. I *believed* that God was good, but if God is good, why are so many innocent people suffering? I *believed* that I should forgive seventy

> WE MUST *WITHDRAW TO ENGAGE* IF OUR INTERACTION WITH THE WORLD IS TO BEAR ANY FRUIT THAT LASTS.

times seven (Matthew 18:21-22), but forgiveness was getting more and more difficult for me. I *believed* that God loved me, but I was terribly afraid I might do something or believe something that would separate me from God forever.

Consequently, as I took time to withdraw from the business of trying to save the world, these kinds of contradictions in my lived experience were exposed. I was sorely uprooted from the ground of being. Consequently, my actions in the world, no matter how noble they might have seemed, lacked vitality. Instead of drawing from the ground of being and aligning with the heart of existence, I was functioning alone in the world. My isolation was marked with a separate self who would call on God as needed. That's much different from being rooted in the presence of God in whom I live and move and have my being (Acts 17:28). I wanted to be aligned with the very heart of existence.

Not only did my life and work lack vigor, it was limited in its capacity to bear lasting fruit. The work drained me. Yes, I was passionate about it. I believe I was even called to it. But since I wasn't well grounded in the source of all life, much of the energy offered to the work was mine alone, and my energy is limited. God's, on the other hand, is boundless.

When we are rooted in the ground of being and aligned with the heart of existence, there's a different source of energy flowing through us. That doesn't mean I don't get physically tired. But withdrawing for daily contemplative prayer and longer periods of retreat frees up a lot of energy. The interior static noise of our happiness programs limits vitality. Contemplative practice reduces that noise and helps us become more cooperative with the divine will. Through contemplative prayer we get in the flow of what God is already doing in and through us. It's less about our *effort* and more about our *alignment* with the divine.

Curiously, alignment with the divine has been the focal point of my present life for quite some time. That morning my neck locked up, I was really concerned. I had experienced neck and back pain off and on for years, but it had always worked itself out. I thought my massage therapist could help. But there was no relief after an hour of intense massage on my neck.

Out of desperation, I ended up in the chiropractor's office. Results of the tests revealed my C-2 vertebra was pushed out of alignment because of systemic issues in my middle and lower back. My thoracic spine was compromised with the onset of degenerative disc disease and arthritis. My lumbar spine was completely misaligned, and my left hip was rotated. Due to minor accidents during childhood and adult injury and stress, at forty-four years old, my spine had reached the limits of compensation. Major correction was prescribed to bring my back into healthy alignment to alleviate current complications and prevent future health problems and disability.

I'm convinced there's a spiritual dimension to everything in life. As my physical body becomes more aligned, I'm experiencing the clarity and vitality for which I've been longing. That vivacity helps me to live more fully into my soul's purpose. Consider whatever physical, emotional, or mental challenges you may be facing, and let go of being in control. It's not about being perfectly well or perfectly physically fit. God is at work in you and through you—even in your limitations. All that is required of you is cooperation with what is.

Let me say it again: Let go. Dare to fall into the grace of God that is always with us. Go ahead. Take a trust fall. I guarantee you will not only be caught, but you'll be transformed. And with every act of trust-filled withdrawal into grace, you will be better aligned to cooperate with God in the healing of our world.

Trustfully withdrawing into divine grace is nothing less than what Jesus taught by example. He knew the importance of withdrawing from the crowds and the needs of others to be in prayer. That scene in the Garden of Gethsemane, shortly before his arrest and impending crucifixion (Luke 22:39-53) is so revealing. As he stayed awake through the night to pray, he was confronted with his false self—the self that is prone to attach to power and control, affection and esteem, and security and survival. But he was being called to transcend those attachments and inhabit his true self—the self that is a part of something bigger than his personality structure, the self that is packed with purpose and destiny.

As he prayed, he was no doubt wrestling with his inner demons—not so unlike us. Scripture states that he was in such agony in his prayer that he sweat drops of blood. This is the kind of prayer that unlocks power and potential to change the world, because it first changes us.

One of the most defining aspects of what sets contemplative prayer apart from other forms of prayer is its *power to change the one praying*. It is transformational prayer. As we learn how to dispose ourselves to the interior work of God through contemplative prayer, we are freed, healed, and empowered to engage the world with life-giving impact. Yielding to such a work of grace requires us to withdraw for periods of solitude. But make no mistake, withdrawing from the world does not remove us from its need. Periods of withdrawal make our interactions with the world more effective.

> WHAT SETS CONTEMPLATIVE PRAYER APART FROM OTHER FORMS OF PRAYER IS ITS *POWER TO CHANGE THE ONE PRAYING.*

This was the lesson I began to learn by osmosis as I spent time at the Abbey of Gethsemani. The influence of Thomas Merton oozes out of that sacred place. There really is no better luminary for such a lived reality.

A SOCIALLY ENGAGED HERMIT

The 1950s were a crucial time in US history, and certainly throughout the world. World War II had ended in 1945, and American society was shaken to the core. Those times revealed the mass brutality and destruction of which humanity was capable. America emerged on the scene as a global military power with frightening potential. The possibility of nuclear annihilation hung over the planet like a doomsday cloud. Fear was palpable, and people were looking for meaning. This was also when the civil rights movement moved into mainstream society. Social unrest was undeniable. The nation needed leaders to give hope for a better world. Thomas Merton was one such icon.

Merton was a leading force in renewing the contemplative tradition for the Christian West. Some credit him with almost single-handedly renewing the tradition for our time. Revered as one of the greatest spiritual masters of the twentieth century, he is arguably the most influential Christian author of his time. His bestselling autobiography, *The Seven Storey Mountain,* was published in 1948 when Merton was just thirty-three years old. The publisher planned to print 7,500 copies but pre-sold more than 20,000. By 1984 sales exceeded three million, and the book has remained continuously in print. It has been translated into over twenty languages. Not only was it on the *National Review's* list of the 100 best nonfiction books of the century, but it was also included in *100 Books That Changed the Century (2000)* by William J. Petersen. Reviewers liken his work to Augustine's *Confessions*. Undoubtedly, he is a significant teacher for helping us navigate the contemplative journey.

I had heard of Merton when I was at university, since his monastery was located a little over an hour away. But I knew very little about him and never visited the abbey during that time. Later I came to know Dan Connelly, one of the kindest men you would ever meet. Strong yet gentle, he is a "salt of the earth" kind of man. He told me that Merton's book *The Seven Storey Mountain* was the best book he ever read. He remarked how it changed his life—like so many other people, I later came to realize. It was Merton's story that inspired Dan to consider becoming a Catholic priest. He courageously went to seminary before realizing that wasn't to be his vocation.

Merton was born in Prades, France, in 1915. Both of his parents were artists. His mother was from the United States, and his father was from New Zealand. The origin of his life seemed destined for fecundity. As magical as an artist's home could be, sadly, Merton's childhood was marked with tragedy and instability. When he was only six years old, his mother died from cancer. Just ten years later, his father died of a brain tumor. But in spite of his troubled upbringing, he was privileged to study at both Cambridge and Columbia.

The son of artists, Merton was a colorful figure, well acquainted with his humanity. It's no secret that as a young man he was known for his indiscretions with women. In fact, one relationship led to the conception of a daughter. In those times, conceiving a child outside of marriage was a shameful social scandal. So, he was persuaded to leave England, and that's when he ended up in America at Columbia. Later in life, while a monk, there was another scandal—a love affair between

Merton and his nurse. As for his daughter, sadly, she was killed during the German air raids on London.

The Merton the world came to know was a monk who had taken strict vows of stability, fidelity, obedience, and silence. But Merton was not immune to the passions and sufferings that make us human. He had a voracious hunger for life, truth, and love. His insatiable appetite drove him to a relentless pursuit of God. He wrote,

> The Christian solitary does not seek solitude merely as an atmosphere or as a setting for a special and exalted spirituality. Nor [do they] seek solitude as a favorable means for obtaining something [they] want—contemplation. [They] seek solitude as an expression of [their] total gift of [themselves] to God.[8]

By the time he was twenty-six years old, Merton joined the Abbey of Our Lady of Gethsemani, in Trappist, Kentucky, where I came to learn of him fifty years later. Some years after writing his autobiography, Merton confessed that his decision to become a monk was as much a "no" to the social violence of the time (war, racial injustice, and inexorable consumerism) as it was a "yes" to the goodness of humanity and a pursuit of the Absolute.

Tragically, Merton died in a very ill-fated accident in Bangkok in 1968. He was in Thailand attending an interfaith dialogue between Catholic and non-Catholic monks. After one of the meetings, he went back to his room to rest, and when he stepped out of the bath, he was electrocuted by a nearby fan. An avid peace activist, his body ironically was flown back to the States on a US military aircraft returning from war in Vietnam. He is buried at the Abbey of Gethsemani. His grave is marked with his ordained priesthood name etched into the stone: Father Louis.

His autobiography undeniably awakened Western Christian consciousness. It resonated with a people in search of meaning. Americans at that time were recovering from a lot of violence. They faced the increasing threat of worldwide destruction due to the production of atomic bombs and nuclear weapons. And they wrestled with the injustices of racism and discrimination that plagued the nation. Merton's life and story offered hope for a people in despair. But the best of his writing was yet to come.

He was, in fact, an inexhaustible writer, producing over sixty books and hundreds of articles covering the topics of spirituality and social justice. He became known for his interfaith dialogues and taking a stand for nonviolent resistance during the 1960s race riots and the Vietnam War. Far from being irrelevant in his chosen contemplative vocation, his choice to withdraw into cloistered life was in fact an option to engage the concerns of his time with pointed relevancy.

James Finley, who learned from Merton for six years as a monk in Gethsemani, says Merton would tell him, "We don't come to the monastery to get away from suffering; we come to hold the suffering of all the world."[9]

WITHDRAWING TO ENGAGE

Merton illuminates for us the possibility of integrating contemplation with action. He demonstrates the power of withdrawing so that we can engage with effectiveness. In fact, the more Merton withdrew from the world, the more he courageously confronted the horrific injustices of his time such as poverty, war, violence, and consumerism.

Staying true to the reality that our true self is not only connected to God but to all people, Merton helps us see that true contemplation is not divorced from action. The more united we are to God in prayer, the more naturally that source flows out from its inner spring, becoming a stream of action in relationship to others.[10] To abide in this "spring" and let the living waters of Christ flow freely through us, we must be committed to regular contemplative prayer. There really is no other way.

One of the things I appreciate most about Merton is how he understood the direct connection between inner transformation and the healing of society. An admirer of Gandhi and his nonviolent political revolution, Merton wrote, "The whole Gandhian concept of nonviolent action and *satyagraha* is incomprehensible if it is thought to be a means of achieving unity rather than as the fruit of inner unity already achieved."[11]

If the Christian contemplative life was once seen as disconnected from the active life, that changed with Merton. Though he took the strict vows of a Cistercian (Trappist) monk, retreating to the rural hills of the Bluegrass State, often residing as a hermit, Merton was not withdrawn from the world. In solitude, Merton journeyed to the ground of his being and found not only God but the world as well. From this unified ground, Merton accessed his deepest self and found himself connected to all people in the struggle to build a better world.

SOLITUDE CONFRONTS THE FALSE SELF

Solitude is essential preparation for transformation. "Solitude," says Merton, "is necessary for spiritual freedom."[12] Aptly, Merton describes different kinds of solitude: physical and interior. Physical solitude is helpful in that it assists us in detaching from external distractions. It is the first step toward being predisposed for transformation. But it's the *interior* solitude that is crucial. "There is no true solitude except interior solitude."[13] Merton says,

> While physical solitude removes us from our fellow man, interior solitude unites us with him. It is communion with our fellow man on a much deeper level than the social fictions of life in a large city or a technological world allow.[14]

External solitude serves only to support interior solitude. Once one becomes adept at cultivating interior solitude, then one finds it easier to maintain it when engaged in daily life with others. Still, the regular practice of solitude is nonnegotiable for ongoing transformation of the false self.

Merton is in fact credited for the widely used terminology *true self* and *false self*. Other helpful terms include *old self, new self; large self, small self; separate self; unified self; essential self; non-essential self; floating self; grounded self. Transcendent self* and *essence* are also used to describe the true self. Merton's description of the true self is notably expressed in his book *Conjectures of a Guilty Bystander*:

> At the center of our being is a point of nothingness which is untouched by sin and by illusion, a point of pure truth, a point or spark which belongs entirely to God, which is never at our disposal, from which God disposes of our lives, which is inaccessible to the fantasies of our own mind or the brutalities of our own will. This little point of nothingness and of *absolute poverty* is the pure glory of God in us.... It is like a pure diamond, blazing with the invisible light of heaven. It is in everybody, and if we could see it we would see these billions of points of light coming together in the face and blaze of a sun that would make all the darkness and cruelty of life vanish completely.[15]

The false self, Merton says, is an illusory person. "Every one of us is shadowed by an illusory person: a false self. This is the person that I want myself to be but who cannot exist, because God does not know anything about him."[16]

Merton describes the false self as the empirical self, outer self, ego-self, external self, superficial self, Cartesian self, collective self, and technological self.[17] Descartes's age-old assertion *Cogito, ergo sum,* "I think, therefore I am," fuels the false self. This false self makes humanity and God objects to be manipulated for self-interest. *I* is the center of all reality, who imprisons the true self, keeping the real self isolated and out of touch with others. In our unawakened state, we are in exile from our own spiritual depth. The false self is alienated.

Merton contrasts profoundly with Descartes, pointing to the reality that our thoughts can in fact deceive us. We are not who we *think* we are. We live an illusion of identity, an identity crisis of which we are unaware. We identify with this false self, and without contemplation we never wake up and discover our true self.

Merton further illuminates how the false self relates to sin:

Every one of us is shadowed by an illusory person: a false self. . . .
My false and private self is the one who wants to exist outside
the reach of God's will and God's love—outside of reality and
outside of life. And such a self cannot help but be an illusion. . . .
All sin starts from the assumption that my false self, the self that
exists only in my own egocentric desires, is the fundamental
reality of life to which everything else in the universe is ordered.[18]

The false self is over-identified with programs for happiness. My false
self identifies most strongly with the happiness program "affection
and esteem." When I have an overly emotional reaction to circumstances or a person, I can be pretty sure this program for happiness has been triggered. Let me be clear. The *need* for esteem, security,
or control is not the sin. The need is basic to our humanity. It's the
attachment to gratifying the need that is the sin.

The attachment to my need to be esteemed in just the right way is
the shape of my false self and is what motivates me to sin. My false
self is insecure. She doesn't know that she is loved and so she craves
reinforcement from others. She lives outside of the reality of being the
beloved of God—always loved and accepted no matter what. This part
of me lives alienated from God's will and God's love. She attempts to
gratify her need apart from the embrace of divine love. Her desire to
be esteemed and approved is central, and her motivations revolve
around feeding that desire. When people or circumstances frustrate
that gratification, an emotional reaction is certain.

For example, one day my husband and I were having a heated conversation. I was not comfortable with him doing something that he
wanted to do. I expressed my resistance, and he expressed his resistance
to my resistance. He didn't immediately accept my position. We were at
a standoff. After a couple decades of marriage, we've learned that when
we're both tired and stressed, it's better to give time and space for difficult
conversations. So I went about the rest of my evening waiting for a more

opportune time to resolve the tension between us. It wasn't long until I experienced anxiety and fear and an outburst of tears. My false self had taken over. My husband's raw and honest display of his own emotions caused my false self to become insecure and flooded with extremely negative thoughts that only later came to consciousness: *Maybe he really doesn't love me after all. Maybe he doesn't want to be with me.*

This is a pattern for me. It surfaces over and over again in various relationships and life circumstances. I've come to know my false self. Often, I can see her coming, but not always. She is terribly egocentric. Everything revolves around her being stroked by others in just the right way to reassure her that she is loved. This is the shape of my false self. This may seem relatively harmless, but we mustn't be deceived. When the false self goes unchecked and unaccountable, it can lead to violence.

The false self is in fact the source of violence, for it is motivated to gratify its need for power and control, affection and esteem, or security and survival at all costs. According to Merton,

> People who know nothing of God, and whose lives are centered on themselves, imagine that they can only find themselves by asserting their own desires and ambitions and appetites in a struggle with the rest of the world. They try to become real by imposing themselves on other people, by appropriating for themselves some share of the limited supply of created goods and thus emphasizing the difference between themselves and other men who have less than they, or nothing at all.[19]

When our false self is the predominant self, violence is played out in relationships between individuals, communities, and nations. The ultimate cure for peace is nurturing oneness with God and with all humanity through contemplation. Merton says, "Since our inmost 'I' is the perfect image of God, then when that 'I' awakens, he finds within himself the Presence of Him Whose image he is."[20]

The true self knows restraint because at its Source is enough affection and esteem, security and survival, and power and control. There is always enough when we are in God. The true self is rooted in the ground of being from which flows an awareness of being loved, safe, and having no need to fear. Therefore, the true self doesn't need to force people and circumstances to manufacture reassurance of having enough affection, security, and power. We possess everything we need by our connection with the Source of our existence. The false self, therefore, is fundamentally a slave to fear. The true self is free and unafraid.

The false self finds its identity in circumstances and other people, which leaves the false self terribly insecure and attached to the things of this world. The true self finds its identity in God. Merton affirms, "The secret of my identity is hidden in Him. He alone can make me who I am, or rather who I will be when at last I fully begin to be. But, unless I desire this identity and work to find it with him and in him, the work will never be done."[21]

> THE TRUE SELF FINDS ITS IDENTITY IN GOD.

In solitude, silence, and stillness, Merton examined his false self with its self-will and resistance to God. And out of solitude he emerged more rooted in his true self, able to engage the world in a way that offered hope and meaning to the people of his time. His influence is still very much at work today, fifty years after his death.

Merton's writings take a deep dive into the contemplative dimension of life and faith where he helps us navigate the journey. Step by step with Merton by our side, we find the ground of being beneath us, stabilizing us. Through Merton we find courage to withdraw into spiritual practice and the grace to engage a fractured and hurting world with substantial hope and relevant action.

Today, we face socio-political and environmental concerns equal to if not greater than the concerns of Merton's time. The US faces the effects of unrepentant history connected with the exploitation, oppression, violence, and unjust treatment of persons of color. Unaccountable capitalism has laid waste to sacred lands and dishonors political treaties. Unbridled consumerism threatens to buy anything—even the bodies of men, women, and children for labor, including sex labor. Nuclear war is still a very real global threat. Mother Earth cries out her distress through climate change. It's the most vulnerable creatures of our planet, including people in poverty, who suffer the most from our collective unconscious.

For the sake of our global family and the planet we call home, we must learn how to creatively withdraw so we can be more aligned with the divine will in co-creating the world we all want to live in—a world in which we are loved, safe, and have no need to fear.

The challenges seem insurmountable. With such tremendous brokenness in the world we must learn to be present. Developing the capacity to be present begins by making time to withdraw. It's crucial to make time for solitude during regular contemplative prayer or for longer stretches of time on retreat. In doing so, we learn to be present to our own suffering, which allows us to be present to the suffering around us. When we can be present to our pain, we open to the grace of transforming it. And like Father Richard frequently says, "If we do not transform our pain, we will most assuredly transmit it."[22]

The best way I've found to be present is to return to conscious breath. Such a simple, yet life-altering, act. Following Merton's lead, take time to withdraw from your active life for a moment. In solitude, take a big, deep breath and sink into yourself. Dare to contend with your inner turmoil, open to God's healing. From there, you'll be more equipped to engage the troubled world around you.

Practice: Breath Prayer

The breath prayer helps us to be present and is fitting given Merton's appreciation for Eastern Orthodoxy. The Eastern church maintained Christianity's contemplative dimension much better than the Western church, holding the doctrine of *theosis*, or divinization, central throughout the centuries. *Theosis* emphasizes what church father Irenaeus affirmed as early as the second century: "God passed into man so that man might pass over to God."[23] Christian contemplation hinges on the affirmation that by grace we are partakers in the divine nature (2 Peter 1:4). The breath prayer, like all contemplative prayer practices, helps us live into that divine nature and be a channel for love and mercy in our world.

Breath prayer is an ancient Christian prayer practice dating back to at least the sixth century. Historically, it is associated with the Greek and Russian Orthodox churches, and known as the Jesus Prayer or Prayer of the Heart. Early practitioners would repeat to the rhythm of their breath the phrase, "Lord Jesus Christ, Son of God, have mercy on me, a sinner." In time, the prayer was shortened to, "Lord Jesus Christ, have mercy" or simply, "Jesus, mercy."

Breath prayer is an example of "praying without ceasing," as the apostle Paul admonished us to do (1 Thessalonians 5:17), and has the potential to become as natural as breathing. It is intended to be a very short prayer of praise or petition, just six to eight syllables. The words of the prayer can be easily adjusted to your heart's desire.

Praise is expressed by invoking one of the divine names such as Yahweh, God, Jesus, Lord, Father, Mother, Christ, or Spirit on the in-breath. You may prefer another name of adoration. Your request, intention, or praise is composed of the few words following the initial divine invocation and prayed on the out-breath.

Breath prayer is usually recited silently. But some people sing it; others chant it. It's your prayer; pray it your way.

You may use breath prayer on the go or as the method for your daily spiritual practice in stillness. When praying in stillness, repeat the prayer over and over to the rhythm of your breath. Keep your attention on the words of the prayer, like a mantra. If your attention wanders, gently return to the words of the prayer. Eventually, the words may fall away, the mind becomes still, and you are brought into deeper contemplation.

Begin with five minutes and gradually increase the time to fifteen or twenty minutes as you become disciplined with the prayer. You may want to use a timer to free yourself from watching the clock. Afterward, some find it useful to write in a journal their experience with the prayer.

To begin, close your eyes and recall the line "Be still and know that I am God" (Psalm 46:10). Be still, calm, peaceful, open to the presence of God.

With your eyes closed, imagine that God is calling you by name. Imagine that God is actually asking, "(Your name), what do you want?" As with the blind man on the road to Jericho (Luke 18:35), Jesus kindly looks you in the eyes and asks, "What do you want from me?"

Give God a simple and direct answer that comes honestly from your heart. Your answer may be one word such as *peace* or *love* or *help*. It may be several words or a phrase such as, "Show me the way," or "Give me peace." Whatever your answer, it is the foundation of your breath prayer. Perhaps you simply want to praise God or express gratitude. Your prayer may be something simple like "I adore you," or "Thank you."

Select the name that you are most comfortable using to invoke God's presence. Combine it with your request or praise. This is your prayer.

Breathe in your invocation for God. Breathe out your request or praise.

You may need to compose several prayers before you find one that truly arises from your deepest desire. So, look carefully at your prayer. Does it reflect the heart of your desire? There's no limit to developing your breath prayer. It may be the same from day to day, or it may change.

Sometimes you may want to reverse the practice. Sit in silence and let the Spirit pray through you. Ask for God to reveal *your* name and *God's desire* for you. Consider Isaiah 62:2: "You will have a new name that YHWH's mouth will bestow." This can be a profound experience. You may wind up hearing something like, "Beloved, you are good," or "Child, rest." Wait on God and see how you may be renewed.

Sample Breath Prayers

- Jesus, free me.
- Lord, show me the way.
- Holy one, heal me.
- Jesus, have mercy.
- Holy Wisdom, guide me.
- Father/Mother (Abba/Amma), let me feel your presence.

For more information visit gravitycenter.com/practice/breath-prayer.

CHAPTER THREE

FINDING LIBERATION BY DISCERNMENT

*And when you turn to the right and when you
turn to the left, your ears will hear a voice behind
you saying, "This is the way—walk in it."*

ISAIAH 30:21

*Little by little he came to recognize
the difference between the spirits that agitated
him, one from the enemy and one from God.*

ST. IGNATIUS OF LOYOLA

WHILE WE ARE AFFORDED various opportunities to express ourselves and be of service to others, how do we know what the best choice is? How can we be certain of our purpose and how to enact that purpose in our vocation? How can we navigate well all of the disparate voices in our head *and* in our community? And how can we determine the *best* option in a sea of good ones?

Western society is the most socially, politically, and economically progressive in history. We have generous access to education and information, opportunity, and the so-called free market. With such liberties, we grow up believing we can have anything we want and be anything we want to be.

At the touch of a button we can engage more than ever with the global landscape of possibility. Back in 2012 the Pew Internet and

American Life Project found that 95 percent of teens ages twelve through seventeen were internet users, 76 percent used social networking sites, and 77 percent had cell phones. Among those ages eighteen through twenty-nine, 96 percent were online, 84 percent used social networking sites, and 97 percent had cell phones. Well over half of that age group had smartphones, and 23 percent owned tablet computers like iPads.[1] I imagine these numbers have only increased since this data was collected. This virtually unlimited connection to the world gives us access to information and opportunity that our grandparents never imagined.

With such prospects comes the possibility and responsibility to respond to a world plagued by war, disparity, the violation of human rights, and ecological destruction. But the myriad of options for engagement can be overwhelming and paralyzing. More and more so-called hyper-connected (in the digital sense) people are struggling to purposefully connect to anything meaningful. Perhaps you also find yourself overwhelmed by information overload and paralyzed by an array of choices. Knowing your purpose and discerning what to say yes to and what to say no to begins with discovering who you are.

WHO AM I? WHY AM I HERE?

I know more than one person today who has tattooed on their body the quote from J. R. R. Tolkien's poem in *The Lord of the Rings*: "Not all those who wander are lost." True. But it seems society has raised up a generation who are *aimlessly* wandering. To be lost is to be disconnected from a point of orientation, without a center of gravity. Similarly, aimless wandering—not knowing from where you come and not really knowing where you're headed—is no way to live.

Jesus' message was about living an abundant life, a meaningful life. Wandering is hardly abundant; it lacks focus. Today it is rare to come across a person who is focused on their purpose in life. This lack of single-mindedness points back to the question of identity.

The average person in today's society has no idea who she or he is, let alone what their purpose is. Without a rooted identity, one's agency is terribly compromised. Many of us are imprisoned by perceived notions of freedom, but discernment holds the key to authentic liberation of identity.

If you don't know who you are, how can you know what it is you are meant to do with your life? The question raises another question: How can you find out who you are?

Contemplative spirituality holds the answer to these fundamental questions. Discernment through meditation addresses the lack of identity and purpose plaguing so many. I like how my friend Stuart puts it: "Discernment is a conscious judgment grounded in awareness of our deepest identity in God."

In my life, discernment has always been key to unlocking meaning. Experiences of life-changing discernment came into play when I decided where to attend college, when I chose to marry my husband, when I determined to accept leadership for the social justice organization we were a part of, and in a number of other very difficult decisions made along the way.

Within weeks of graduating university, I found myself in India. For the next twenty years, I served with a dynamic international community among people in poverty. I inherited leadership of this missional community, alongside Chris, at the young age of twenty-two.

Discernment was critical when Chris and I chose to leave that organization and the community we had helped build and lead for the better years of our young adulthood. True, we had grown beyond that organization in a lot of ways. Most especially, we had come to appreciate the necessity of integrating contemplation and action. The organization limited our capacity to fully express that. But we had worked so hard to build that community. It offered a degree of security, control, and esteem. To say it wasn't easy to walk away from it is an understatement. We didn't know who we were apart from it.

All we had was a mustard seed of vision for what is now Gravity. We wondered, *Would anyone be interested in learning about contemplative spirituality? Would anyone want to attend a retreat with us?* At that point, I hadn't even completed my master's in Christian spirituality or certificate in spiritual direction, training that was crucial to our new endeavor. I wondered if I was really well enough prepared to make such a career change.

Making important life decisions like this is challenging because there are usually conflicting voices in our head. In my experience, there are at least three: my true self, my false self, and the voice of someone else whom I'm tempted to try and please or obtain approval from. It's hard enough to distinguish between my true and false self. Placating to what I think others want from me just makes matters worse. Discernment, or discerning spirits, is an art form. But before it becomes a masterpiece, it's more like finger painting—you just figure it out as you go.

In the beginning, discernment doesn't come easily. It feels like tension. A decision must be made, but we're not sure which decision is best. Opposing possibilities pull us in different directions. One option sometimes feels better than another, but choosing only what feels good isn't necessarily the best choice. Sometimes, what our truest self demands feels scary. At those times, we are being invited to grow and stretch the boundaries of who we think we are and what we're capable of.

Cultivating discernment, the capacity to know who we are and what our purpose is, is at the heart of contemplative spirituality. The best of contemplative spirituality liberates us to know the essence of our identity *and* motivates us to give our best selves to a world in need. Uncovering our identity requires a spirituality that integrates both contemplation *and* action. Thankfully, Ignatius of Loyola provides just that. He is one of the greatest teachers in the contemplative

> CONTEMPLATIVE SPIRITUALITY LIBERATES US TO KNOW THE ESSENCE OF OUR IDENTITY.

tradition to shine light on what is an otherwise obscure path to becoming.

A MASTER OF DISCERNMENT

Unlike most Christian mystics who chose a cloistered life, Ignatius opted for the "mixed life"—to be in the world (active) while staying committed to transformational prayer (contemplation).

Born in 1491 in Azpeitia, Spain, Ignatius was the youngest of thirteen children. His mother died soon after his birth, so he was raised by the local blacksmith's wife. He adopted the surname de Loyola in reference to the Basque village of Loyola where he was born. He died at age sixty-five in Rome.

Ignatius of Loyola was a man before his time. His enlightened perspective on the transformation of the human person rivals modern psychology and human development theory—fields of study unknown in his time. An adventuresome, worldly man of his day, Ignatius came from Basque nobility and passionately pursued his ego's desires until his indulgences got the better of him.

During the Battle of Pamplona in 1521, Ignatius was terribly injured when he was hit in the knee with a cannonball. Can you imagine? Subsequently, he was stripped of his independence and restricted to a convalescent bed. Though incredibly frustrating, this imposed confinement became a portal to greater personal liberation, the kind of freedom we all need. During his recovery, he devoured Holy Scripture and books about the saints. This was the beginning of his conversion. He was subsequently *freed from* his false self in the royal court, his womanizing and self-aggrandizing self. And he was *freed for* a heroic call to spirituality and mission. He was especially inspired by the life of Francis of Assisi. His response to the grace he encountered in that recovery bed resulted in the establishment of a religious order called the Society of Jesus, whose members are referred to as Jesuits. Within his lifetime, the order had reached up to a thousand members, stretching from India to Brazil. Five hundred years later, the order is still thriving and relevant to the needs of our time.

Ignatius's radical conversion transformed his entire being—intellectual mind, emotional soul, and willful body. Having lived to tell of such a total alteration of his person, Ignatius's personal change offers a school of conversion for seekers today.

Though he lived more than five hundred years ago, Ignatius's spirituality is as pertinent today as it was then. His teaching appeals to all people who are committed to spiritual growth.

Ignatius is known for his brilliant, comprehensive book, the *Spiritual Exercises,* a formation program to help seekers experience christological transformation. Ignatian spirituality is chiefly centered on discernment—uncovering the presence and action of God in one's life, and growing in the ability to respond to that presence and action. At the end of this chapter, we'll explore a bit of Ignatius's school of discernment through his prayer of examen.

HEARING THE VOICE OF GOD

Once we have a sense of who we are, we're on the path to discovering that for which we've been created. Sadly, so many things in our culture distract us from our purpose. The internet, social media, smartphones, and tablets can be tools to guide and support us in our created destiny to be agents of creative love in the world. But more often, online surfing serves to confuse our identity and distract us from meaningful agency.

Moreover, addiction to technological stimuli is a very real possibility that undermines the redemptive use of time. It fosters instant gratification, making focused, enduring, purpose-filled self-giving an immense challenge, if not impossible. We struggle to live into an experience of meaningful interconnection and co-creativity with God. It's already difficult enough to overcome selfish, ego-driven ambitions. Add to this impediment manufactured obstacles, and the possibility for doing something beautiful for God and neighbor looks bleak. It's no wonder that all the digital noise in our life deafens us to the voice of God.

Have you ever done something and later regretted it? Maybe it felt morally wrong and had dramatic consequences, or maybe it was subtler, not necessarily a moral evil, and it just didn't "feel right" to you. Paul put it so well when he said, "I don't understand what I do—for I don't do the things I want to do, but rather the things I hate" (Romans 7:15). Ignatius would say that this kind of behavior is *disordered*.

If we're honest with ourselves, when we make choices and behave in ways that are disconnected from the essence of love, we experience unsettledness inside, a sense of disorder. Disorder shows up in our mind in the form of troubled thoughts, in our emotions in the form of feelings like fear, anger, frustration, and sadness, or in our body in the form of tension. Contemplative prayer exposes these disordered attachments and brings order by aligning us with the divine will.

For me, the internal disorder usually manifests first in my body as tension in my neck, jaw, face, or back, or as an upset stomach. Other times it surfaces in emotions—frustration, anger, anxiety, or sadness— and sometimes, directly in my thoughts. Because body wisdom and emotional consciousness tend to be neglected or ignored in our society, I have had to learn to pay attention to my body and emotions when they're trying to speak to me. I often remind myself: "Phileena, listen to your body."

Our bodies have an innate intelligence. They detect being misaligned with God's loving desires, often before it registers in our mind. When these uncomfortable bodily sensations, emotions, or thoughts arise, often instead of paying attention, we do whatever we can to avoid or escape the nagging "voice." Technological stimuli, entertainment, relationships, and alcohol and drugs can all serve as numbing agents for the discomfort and as distractions to the voice of God in our life. The more we neglect and ignore the voice, the duller our sense of hearing becomes. Before long, we grow deaf, and obedience to the loving will of God is then out of reach.

Contemplative spirituality is about obedience flowing from love—obedience to our Creator, who is love, who has a unique life purpose for each of us. But *obedience* has a lot of negative connotations in our culture, so it can be helpful to get back to the Latin root of the word. One of the greatest spiritual writers of our time, Henri Nouwen, helps us redefine and celebrate obedience. During his lifetime, he presented the option for us to live either an obedient or an absurd life. In his lectures and writings, he pointed out that the Latin word *audire,* from which the English word *obedience* is derived, means "to listen or to hear." The Latin word *surdus,* from which the English word *absurd* is derived, means "deaf." It follows that an obedient life is one that hears the voice of God, while an absurd life is deaf to the voice of God.[2] Contemplative spirituality has the potential to make the deaf hear.

In an effort to open our ears, Ignatius offers rules for discernment to guide us. He distinguishes between two. The first rule is for the beginning of the spiritual journey, when we are mostly concerned with choosing what is morally good as opposed to evil. The second rule is for discernment when we have progressed to a point where choosing right and wrong comes quite easily. At this point, the more challenging quest is choosing the best between two goods—choosing what is *particularly* important for my unique purpose in the service of God and others.

A hallmark of Ignatian spirituality is the affirmation that God is present in our desires or the *motions* we experience. When we are led in a way that is true to our path or our created purpose, we may experience motions all across the spectrum, from joy to fear. When we are led in a direction that is in opposition to our path, we may experience the same spectrum of motions. If this is the case, what hope is there for us? The key to finding God in our desires is the art of discernment.

Ignatius writes of the need for "rules to aid us toward perceiving and then understanding, at least to some extent, the various motions which are caused in the soul: the good motions that they may be received, and the bad that they may be rejected."[3] The tricky thing is that "good" and "bad" *motions* are not necessarily good and bad *feelings* as we think of them. Ignatius would define a good motion as that which leads us toward our created purpose and a bad motion as that which leads us away from God's purpose for us. Both commonly understood notions of good and bad feelings can either lead us away from or toward God's purpose.

It's from God's love that we live and move and have our being (Acts 17:28). Meditating on God's love establishes inner freedom. That freedom enables one's desires to be ordered or aligned with our highest purpose. Likewise, inner freedom makes it possible for us to recognize and overcome disordered desires, or that which opposes our highest purpose. Discernment frees us to hear the voice of God and commit to God's creative, compassionate, liberating project in the world.

THE COURAGE TO CHOOSE

When we succeed at decluttering digital noise and distractions and grow in the practice of discernment, there's hope that we may be able to ascertain the voice of God and follow God's leading.

That voice is the essence of what is meant by "vocation." The English word *vocation* is derived from the Latin *vocare*, "to call," and *vox*, "voice." The meaning centers on "a voice calling." John Neafsey, a clinical psychologist and senior lecturer in the department of theology at Loyola University Chicago, says, "Vocation is not only about 'me' and my personal fulfillment, but about 'us' and the common good."[4] When we align with that voice, we are able to sort through the countless voices and choices that face us. We can then commit to a *particular* and *unique* expression of the voice calling us.

Some naively judge spiritual practice as selfish, as if private spiritual devotion takes us away from others and focuses us too much on self (navel-gazing). But in actuality, committing to contemplative practice enlarges our capacity to love our neighbor and have meaningful impact in the world. Taking time to practice being grounded in our principal identity as completely and utterly *loved* roots us in *divine love.* From that Source flows the *power of love* to change the world. This is Christ consciousness.

Years ago a dear friend, while working through the challenges of living in one of the poorest, most polluted cities in the world, made a most profound statement: "To get something, you have to give something up." How true. Anyone who has loved knows that love often requires sacrifice. Contemplative spirituality affirms that the sacrifice called for by love is the sacrifice of the false self (Philippians 1:21). Being freed of the false self enables us to make choices based in love: love of self, God, and others.

> BEING FREED OF THE FALSE SELF ENABLES US TO MAKE CHOICES BASED IN LOVE: LOVE OF SELF, GOD, AND OTHERS.

Being firmly established in God's universal and particular love (Ephesians 3:16-19) enables us to be what Ignatius calls "indifferent" to created things. Buddhists refer to this principle as non-attachment. Indifference or non-attachment means to live with interior freedom, letting nothing own us but love. Indifference is not a disinterested, aloof posture to life. Rather, indifference is the liberty to choose what is best, even when it goes against our natural inclinations. In this way, we bravely overcome the false self and live into our true self.

We can then utilize the things of the world to the extent that they help us to live our created purpose and let go of things when they hinder us from that purpose. When rooted in love, we are able to better discern how to courageously live with charity in every thought, choice, decision, and action. To the extent that we absorb God's love, we participate in our created purpose to bring all of creation to its fullness. Ignatius reiterates that the various choices to be made in life are tethered to the ultimate objective to praise, reverence, and serve God and so attain our ultimate fulfillment. Discernment helps us realize which choices will meet that objective.

In the *Exercises*, Ignatius demonstrates how God inspires decisions through our will (body/gut), feelings (heart/emotions), or reason (mind/thoughts).[5] All three ways are reliable, and when we experience the operation of one, the other two can be activated for confirmation. But this process of decision making is only suitable for those who have developed an adequate capacity for interior freedom, indifference, or non-attachment. To discern our highest purpose, we must have the courage to be led wherever the Spirit leads. We must hold a healthy sense of detachment from the things of the world. It's that kind of inner freedom that sometimes gets people killed. Just think of the master Jesus, and great leaders like Gandhi and Martin Luther King Jr.

The spiritual journey begins with the belief that we are children of God called to live a life of meaning. But responding to that call is not only about *being selected* by God but about *self-selection* as well. Being anchored in a deep and rich contemplative spirituality helps us find courage to choose risky endeavors that catalyze transformation in the lives of others.

When we are indifferent, we are free to follow Christ and thus live into our destiny and fulfillment. No longer held captive by countless choices masquerading as freedom, we are liberated by healthy detachment, really free. Decisions are no longer a burden but a bold prospect to allow more of the Christ life, more of love, to flow through us.

DISCERNING GOD'S LEADING
THROUGH SACRED SCRIPTURE

It was a typical hot and sultry Nebraska summer. I had been in discernment concerning the timing of when to launch Gravity, a Center for Contemplative Activism. I felt that I had carried this "baby" to full term; the "delivery date" was the only question left.

I thought I had it figured out. I planned to launch at the beginning of the next year. But then it seemed God's will might be to launch this new initiative sooner. An incredible opportunity to open a space in

September, rather than the following January, presented itself to me, and I needed to make a decision right away.

As I prayed with Scripture, two meditations early on opened the door for me to experience specific graces or gifts that Ignatius says support the spiritual journey: the grace to grasp the completeness of Jesus' gift in his baptism act, and the grace to walk faithfully with Jesus. These experiences deepened my knowledge and love of Jesus and my capacity to follow him more fully.

It was a Tuesday morning when I meditated on all the Gospel accounts of Jesus' baptism. And though I prayed fervently for the grace to comprehend the completeness of Jesus' gift in his baptism (as Ignatius instructs), I experienced nothing. Since I felt that I was praying with a generous and open heart (as Ignatius instructs), I thought that it was okay to move on to the other prayer experiences. Little did I know I would return at a later time to Jesus' baptism, which would be critical for my ongoing conversion.

With the peace to move on at the time, the following morning I meditated on John 2:1-11, the wedding at Cana, taking the passage sentence by sentence and imagining my present circumstances within it. Almost immediately I experienced penetrating insight. I don't often hear direct messages from Scripture concerning my specific life circumstances, but by using Ignatius's way of praying with imagination and all of my senses, on this occasion I did. The following reflection is a vulnerable example of how we can experience grace through sacred text. In this experience, I encountered movements in all three areas of my personhood or intelligent centers: my will, feelings, and reason.

"On the third day." This phrase echoed thoughts of the resurrection of Jesus, and I was invited to consider my current life experience as resurrection. This came on the heels of a few years of much trial, temptation, hardship, and the emotional and spiritual death of my false identity. The invitation to ponder this phrase came as a subtle but energetic pull of my *will* toward this statement.

"The wine ran out." Upon reading this phrase, I was immediately drawn to my twenty-year service in social justice. Up until a few years

prior, "intoxicating fruit" flowed through that expression of my vocation. But recently the dregs had run dry. As I read these words, I experienced a deep *feeling* in my gut that connected to my mind, reasoning how this phrase related to my personal life. In the text, Jesus responded to Mary's request for him to do something about the wine by saying the following line.

"My hour has not yet come." At this point, and each time during the week when I returned to this statement, I deeply identified with Jesus to the point of tears. I too have heard the call to do something for God but thought "the hour" would come later that year. I had been reluctant to respond to the invitation to do something *now*. I identified with Jesus' response to Mary, "My time has not yet come."

"Six stone water-jars for the rites of purification, each holding twenty to thirty gallons." My immediate impression was that the stone jars, for me, represented the purpose to which God was calling me. Several years ago, I had received this call to start a center for contemplative activism (what would become Gravity). In the Gospel story, the purpose of the jars was to provide water for the Jewish rites for purification. My sense was that Gravity would provide "water" for the purification of social action. During this time, I continued to try and pay attention to my thoughts related to these Scriptures.

"Jesus said, 'Fill the jars with water.'" I heard this filtered through my personal circumstances as follows: the "water" poured into Gravity is my lifeblood and that of others who will contribute to its founding. The source of this lifeblood is the Christ life; I am just a vessel by which the life can flow into and through Gravity.

"Everyone serves the good wine first and then the inferior wine after, but you have kept the good wine until now." The personal message I received was that the "intoxicating fruit" that will come out of Gravity will be the miracle and power of God, for God's purposes. "Saving the best wine for last" symbolizes that my work up until now was just the beginning; the best life force and fruit is yet to come.

"Jesus did this, the first of his signs, and revealed his glory, and his disciples believed in him." And I knew that Jesus was doing "all of this" in my life: revealing his glory, confirming, and giving me consolation that I am doing his will. As people see his provision in my life, they too will *believe*—better interpreted as "believe into," "belong," "abide," or "dwell" in God. I experienced a quiet inner knowing that the work of Gravity will help accomplish this.

During a time of facing significant change in my life and pondering the risks I was taking, these reflections felt very consoling. Contemplative spirituality teaches us how to open to such dynamic, personal encounters with God through sacred text.

My experience with this Scripture passage was profound. And I must admit, this isn't an everyday occurrence. In that season, since I had taken regular, deliberate time out to open myself to Scripture, I was especially sensitized. Perhaps this made me available to receive such a personal word for the circumstances of my life during that particular week. But how could I be sure these feelings, thoughts, and motivations were really from God and not from the palak paneer I ate at lunch? Or worse, how could I be sure this wasn't the voice of a dark spirit leading me away from God?

Ignatius is so wise to teach us to pay attention to what we experience in our feelings, intellect, and will. Paying attention is itself prayer. Curiously, Buddhist mindfulness is just that—paying attention. In this way, as we deepen our awareness, we are praying all the time (1 Thessalonians 5:17). Contemplative prayer, like mindfulness, awakens us to listen to what's going on within our body, heart, and mind, and to offer those observations back to God.

CONSOLATIONS AND DESOLATIONS

When we are awake and paying attention to our life, we notice what Ignatius calls consolations and desolations. Simply put, consolations are good moods, while desolations are bad moods.

But though a consolation feels good, it doesn't necessarily mean that it is leading us closer to God's will. Just as a desolation, though it feels bad, does not necessarily mean we are being led away from God's will. Moods are the skin of the soul. We have to get underneath the skin to see which direction the energy is actually flowing.

The soul is made to love and serve God and others. It is the freedom to choose to love and serve God and others with which we are primarily concerned. Since consolations and desolations have the power to move us either toward greater alignment with God's will or further from it, discernment is paramount. But it is a challenging exercise that requires time, patience, and practice. And there's no better teacher for discernment than Ignatius.

My prayer experience with the wedding at Cana is an example of an *intellectual consolation*—a consolation experience that came primarily by way of my reason and imagination. It seemed that I was experiencing consolation for the call to launch Gravity. But Ignatius is prudent to remind us that evil can deceive us with what masquerades as consolations. I wanted to discern more carefully whether this prayer experience was indeed from God to encourage me toward opening the center in September.

Directly following this gift of very personal identification with the story of the wedding at Cana, I began to doubt the experience. Maybe it wasn't time for me to move on from the grace of the first day concerning Jesus' baptism—when I experienced nothing. Maybe I was missing something from the first day that God wanted to reveal to me. Maybe I had proceeded in the prayer exercises too soon. Maybe I had forced these symbols in prayer upon my current circumstances. I wasn't sure what to make of it all. So, I continued to pray that God would either confirm or correct the message I received in meditating on the wedding at Cana. What can be so confusing at times of major decision is that the decision often provokes both consolations and desolations, excitement and anguish.

The challenge of discerning between "two goods" (to open the center in September or January), as opposed to a moral right or wrong, was upon me. Ignatius gives instruction for this challenge of discerning spirits:

> With or by means of a preceding cause, both the good angel and the evil angel are able to cause consolation in the soul, but for contrary purposes. The good angel acts for the progress of the soul, that it may grow and rise from what is good to what is better. The evil angel works for the contrary purpose . . . to entice the soul to his own damnable intention and malice.[6]

I continued to pray every time my mind was drawn to these two strikingly different prayer experiences—the one concerning Jesus' baptism and the one with the wedding at Cana. Wednesday morning it was much of the same for me—no movements when praying for grace related to Jesus' baptism and conflicted motions when praying with the wedding at Cana. When meditating on the wedding at Cana, in addition to the doubts of the previous day, I started hearing: *Who do you think you are? Pretty presumptuous of you to think God would want to use you like this.* I felt accused of being prideful and arrogant.

Later that week I met with my conversation partners Bob and John—during that season we met weekly to unpack our experiences of prayer. That morning, I was feeling discouraged. I had no idea what I would share with them. I felt like I had nothing to offer. But as I asked for their insight about the grace surrounding Jesus' baptism, I took a risk to reveal the contrast in my experience with that meditation and the one on the wedding at Cana. To my surprise, as we shared spiritual conversation I experienced a revelation in my struggle to discern the spirits. John helped me name the emotion of fear, which I realized, in this case, was a sign of the evil spirit.

I was well acquainted with fear and knew this to be true: fear is only helpful if it keeps us from danger. But more often, fear arises from the false self that keeps us from living into our created purpose.

In my own life, fear has often intimidated me from growth. For me, fear has taken the shape of self-abnegation, self-effacement, and hiding from God's calling. You see, my particular upbringing made it difficult for me to properly trust and assert myself as a woman.

Self-abnegation is often the experience of people who have experienced culturally reinforced powerlessness. Like many women in historically male-dominated societies and subcultures, I learned at an early age to quiet my inner voice and hide in the background. While a predominant theme in Christian circles is an admonition to humility, this message is most helpful to those who have experienced power and are prone to pride and superiority. People who have been naturally humbled by inferior circumstances benefit more from the invitation to come out from hiding and trust one's self.

The resistance I experienced to the joy-filled consolation for God's calling and purpose in my life was not new for me. As soon as I could name these things, the tension within me dissipated. I was no longer worried about the first day prayer experience and whether or not I was missing something. I was at peace with the prayer process of the week.

That same morning, Bob introduced me to the spiritual concept of *provo hendi*, Latin for "being brought forward." He gave me the illustration of God pulling me along like a child in a little red wagon. Beautiful. I knew in that moment that was God's action in my life. Through the story of the wedding at Cana and spiritual conversation, I was indeed being invited to get into the "wagon" (Gravity). My time had come. *The* time had come. The Spirit was moving now. The momentum was clear. Following the meeting with Bob and John, I was ready to be childlike, let go, be led, and let God do God's work through me. I was still curious about the grace associated with the meditation on Jesus' baptism, but I let go of trying to control an outcome.

FREE TO LOVE AND SERVE GOD AND OTHERS

A couple of days later, during a lecture on the *Exercises*, the presenter illuminated the gift of Jesus' baptism, and right there in the middle of the presentation, I was overcome with quiet but intense emotion. Suddenly, the experience of the grace I had been praying for all week poured over me—this time through my feelings and emotions. I was deeply moved, and I prayed for the ability to unpack the experience. Ignatius might refer to this experience as a "consolation without cause." He writes,

⌈Only God . . . can give the soul consolation without a preceding cause. For it is the prerogative of the Creator alone to enter the soul, depart from it, and cause a motion in it, which draws the person wholly into love of his Divine Majesty. By "without cause" I mean without any previous perception or understanding of some object by means of which the consolation just mentioned might have been stimulated, through the intermediate activity of the person's acts of understanding and willing.[7] ⌋

Ignatius says that consolation without cause usually occurs when one least expects it, after considerable time has passed between asking for a particular grace and receiving it. Furthermore, the experience of the grace is usually overwhelming. This is exactly what occurred for me that day.

I now felt complete in the prayer exercises. I was free to make a decision to open the center. After a decision is made, it's good to ask God for confirmation. While confirmation may come in the form of felt consolation, it may also be experienced in new, rational thought or an intensification of the will. Overall, confirmation expresses itself in the sense that one has done all one can do to discern God's will and has found it.

Later that day, confirmation came unexpectedly as I meditated on the story of the paralyzed man in Luke 5. Using what Ignatius calls imaginative prayer, I put myself in the role of the paralyzed man and heard Jesus address me directly through the story saying, "Your sin of self-abnegation, which has paralyzed you in the past, is healed. Stand up and walk." This was a deep confirmation to me of the previous grace experiences. I felt more peaceful than ever about launching Gravity sooner rather than later.

Contemplative prayer catalyzed an experience of companioning intimately with Jesus, opening me to receive the graces God wanted to give me so that I could more faithfully partner with God in the world. This is the kind of discernment we can experience through contemplative spirituality.

In an age of hyper-connectivity and inexhaustible access to opportunity, many of us find ourselves imprisoned and paralyzed by endless options posing as freedom. Contemplative spirituality unlocks the gates of our captive souls. By meditating on Scripture and learning to discern spirits, we are schooled in our identity as beloved, we learn how to hear the voice of God, and we obtain courage to choose God's will and live into our truest self.

The prayer of examen—Ignatius's reflective practice of finding God in our desires—is an accessible prayer that can be ritualized in our life as a kind of school for discernment. Taking time each day to examine the motions in our intellect, emotions, and will (thoughts, feelings, and bodily sensations) teaches us how to identify God's leading in our life. We learn to notice the motions that are more conducive to our general and particular created purpose to be loved and to love, and the motions that draw us away from that love. As we pay attention and grow in our ability to listen to these motions, we gradually discern our particular purpose—our unique destiny for living in, through, and for love.

Practice: The Prayer of Examen

The prayer of examen is a grace-filled contemplative practice that opens for us the ability to discern God's will for our lives. It supports us to live from a place of love, giving our love in service of God's project to renew the world—which is our ultimate fulfillment. The practice is quite easy to adopt. Following is a general explanation of the prayer.

The method presented here is adapted from the technique described by Ignatius in his *Spiritual Exercises*. One of the few rules of prayer that Ignatius made for his order was the requirement that Jesuits practice the examen twice daily—at noon and at the end of the day. It's a habit that Jesuits, and many other Christians, practice to this day. There are five steps.

1. Breathe in God's presence.
2. Review the day with gratitude.
3. Give attention to your emotions.
4. Choose one experience of the day and pray with it.
5. Give thanks for God's presence in your day.

Let's look a little more in depth at each step.

1. Breathe in God's presence.
Initiate your adoption of this prayer with a commitment to practice one time daily. Determine if you will practice alone or with a partner, perhaps your spouse or a trusted friend. Whole families can practice the prayer together as well, giving children a head start on learning to discern the presence of God in their life. Begin with a simple prayer of availability to the Holy Spirit. You may want to ritualize your practice by lighting a candle as a symbol of the presence of God, or in another creative manner. Some prefer to practice at the end of the day to allow for a review of the day—perhaps after dinner or before retiring to sleep. Just make sure you don't wait until you're too tired to be alert and present. Another option is to practice in the morning and review the day before.

2. Review the day with gratitude.
Next, review your day silently or in conversation with your partner. Give thanks for everything you can think of to be grateful

for—no matter how bad a day it may have been. Give thanks
for another breath of life, for your physical, mental, emotional,
and spiritual faculties. Be mindful of particular expected or
unexpected gifts from the day. Express your gratitude.

3. Give attention to your emotions.
With a spirit of gratitude intact, notice any emotions that
may arise now as you scanned over your day with gratitude
or that arose earlier in the day. Don't judge them or resist
them. Just let them be. Notice and embrace them.

4. Choose one experience of the day and pray with it.
Notice if there is one feature from the practice thus far that
really grabs your attention. Sit with it and pray with it. It may
be that you are particularly joyful about an opportunity to
serve in a new way. Notice that feeling or idea, and ask God
to lead you toward it or away from it with an attitude of
indifference. Activate your desire to know God's perfect will
for you. Conversely, perhaps you are particularly sad about a
situation in your life. Notice that, and in the same manner ask
God to lead you in that. Perhaps you need God to help you
understand the root of the sadness so that you might not be
blocked from God's perfect will for you in that situation. Stay
with this portion of your prayer until you experience inner
peace. If time does not permit the peace to come, commit to
returning to this stage in the prayer when you have more time.

5. Give thanks for God's presence in your day.
Close your time of prayer with gratitude for God's presence
in every aspect of your day. Pray with a renewed peace and
hope that nothing can separate you from the presence and
love of God.

For more information visit gravitycenter.com/practice
/examen.

CHAPTER FOUR

DISCOVERING DARKNESS IS LIGHT

> *If I say, "The darkness will hide me, and night will be my only light," even darkness won't be dark to you; the night will shine like the day—darkness and light are the same to you.*
>
> PSALM 139:11-12

> *The endurance of darkness is the preparation for great light.*
>
> ST. JOHN OF THE CROSS

HAVE YOU EVER FELT God's absence? Have you had seasons in your life when circumstances were laced with so much pain and suffering that you had no sense of God's presence at all? Perhaps in your growth and development you experienced an identity crisis and were suddenly overwhelmed with emptiness or disorientation. Or maybe you came to a turning point in your spiritual journey. You know, that dubious juncture when doubt and questions about ultimate reality leave you dumfounded. When we experience such ordeals, it can feel as if the ground beneath us is crumbling.

Though these seasons may seem like regression in the spiritual journey, it's actually progress. You see, when we advance spiritually, at times all grows dim. Surprising to some, darkness is a central part of a faithful life.

But before darkness sets in, generally we have learned from experience that God can be trusted, at least to some degree. Deepening trust allows us to give God more access to our life and being. Then the love of God burns stronger and brighter.

The love of God is intense and radiant when it burns. Like a camping log, God alights us with flames. Then, at some point in the journey, God's consuming love obscures that which it's burning. And so, often times when God is at work in our life, we are overcome with the *sense* of darkness. Just as the log is consumed and reduced to ashes, we are overcome.

To allow ourselves to be consumed, we must let go of control and put our trust in the God of love. Letting go to this degree requires our faculties for reason, imagination, feeling, and will to grow dim. So our spiritual life may feel or seem dark and dry. Thus, God may seem absent.

Most of us never imagined that darkness could be the consequence of deepening trust and letting go into God. Unfortunately, for many of us, our religious upbringing communicated the idea that darkness or dryness was an indicator that we had done something to upset God and cause God to withdraw from us. Our insecurity causes us to try and do whatever we can to appease God and invite God's nearness once again.

This way of relating to God stems from a deep-seated theology that God is like the Greek God Zeus, sitting high in the heavens throwing lightning bolts at anyone who makes him angry. It certainly is not the theology that Jesus taught and lived. The God of Jesus was an unconditionally loving and accepting God, like a good father who welcomes the wayward daughter or son back home with open arms and a feast with friends, or a nursing mother who has unconditional compassion for her children. Our image of God profoundly influences our spiritual journey. The more we get acquainted with the God of Jesus, the safer and more inviting the spiritual journey becomes.

It's no wonder we struggle so much in the spiritual journey; we experience ourselves as separated from God. Our misperceptions and false beliefs stand like boulders between us and God. But it's not that God is distant from us; it's that our *awareness* of God's presence is dulled by the interference of our skewed ideas. It's these illusions that have to be dealt with, so that our awareness of God is sharpened. Such surgery has to take place in the dark.

> DARKNESS PLAYS
> A CRUCIAL ROLE
> IN CHRISTIAN
> TRANSFORMATION.

Darkness is necessary if we are to realize we are in God and God is in us—and nothing, absolutely nothing, can separate us from God (Romans 8:38). Most people associate darkness with sin or evil. But, darkness serves to purify our faith and deepen our trust in God. When our spiritual life seems obscure and incomprehensible, we are being weaned from the divine breast (Psalm 131:2), gently nudged away from dependence on sight and certainty. "We walk by faith and not by sight" (2 Corinthians 5:7).

Darkness plays a crucial role in Christian transformation.

WOMB-LIKE DARKNESS

Darkness has been a regular companion for me in the cycles of deepening relationship with God. Usually, suffering of some sort accompanies the lightless season. I've had enough experiences like this now that I've learned not to panic. The first time around, following my crisis of faith in Sierra Leone, I was terrified. I thought something was wrong with me. I thought I must be losing my way. I thought either there is no God or God is so out of reach that I'll never realize God's real presence.

Sure, in my younger life I had had plenty of spiritual experiences. Some I'm sure were authentic. Most were fairly emotional, perhaps some even emotionally manipulated. At any rate, early in the spiritual journey I enjoyed a number of experiences that reinforced God's love for me. But then, the practices that used to help stir up a spiritual experience—worship music, spiritual teaching from the church, Bible reading, and prayer—ran dry. They didn't support my connection with God like they used to. I found myself alone, in obscurity.

Thankfully, the right teachers came into my life and introduced me to contemplative practice as a way of sustaining my faith journey. It's like I was given practices not so much to light the way through the shadows but instead to teach me how to walk in the dark.

During winter seasons in the journey, our spiritual senses are concealed so that our vision for reality can be refined. "Now we see indistinctly, as in a mirror; then we will see face to face. My knowledge is imperfect now; then I will know even as I am known" (1 Corinthians 13:12). In a way, it's like eye surgery. We have to suffer momentary blindness to receive precision of sight.

Years ago, my friends Jeelan and Nazreen gave me the gift of physical sight. Jeelan was born into an Urdu-speaking folk Muslim family in the heart of South India's Tamil Nadu. Nazreen was born into a progressive Pakistani-Malay Muslim family. She grew up in Singapore. When Jeelan moved to Singapore for work, they met, fell in love and eventually married. Today, they are raising their two beautiful children near San Francisco. In all my travels around the world, no one has been more family to me than Naz and Jeel.

I had been nearsighted from the time I was nine years old. I remember as a young student in second or third grade trying to read the classroom chalkboard and using my index fingers to squint my eyes to help make out the teacher's writing. My eyesight used to be so bad that I couldn't see the bedside clock in the morning. As you can imagine, frequent travel to various places around the world made dealing with contact lenses and glasses rather difficult. By the time I was an adult, Lasik corrective eye surgery had come a long way, and I wondered if I would ever be able to afford it. It would be a miracle to have my eyesight restored without the need of corrective lenses.

My friends Nazreen and Jeelan got wind of my desire for the surgery and to my surprise offered to pay for it so I wouldn't have to wait any longer. Imagine. A Muslim gave me, a Christian, sight.

The surgery and recovery were quite an experience. Before the operation, the nurse gave me something to help me relax. Then she secured my eyelids open. The next thing I knew, a laser beam was penetrating my eye. All grew dark. I don't remember a lot after that. When it was time to leave the clinic, patches were put over my eyes. When I returned home, in the dark, unable to see, I could do nothing but sleep. When I woke, it was safe to remove the bandages. I remember the anticipation. Would I really be able to see without my glasses? And sure enough, I could easily read the bedside clock.

Clear sight wasn't exactly instantaneous. It took a little while for my eyes to adjust. I even had to go back to the surgeon for a minor surgical adjustment. It's like this in a spiritual sense too. At times, we have to enter periods of darkness so that God can perform miracles in perception. It's scary. And it requires every ounce of trust we've got. But when the darkness lifts, we see in a new way. There may be an adjustment period, but soon enough we stabilize with new spiritual sight. And in all likelihood, there will be times when we have to enter the darkness again for another adjustment.

In some ways, the role of darkness in the spiritual journey is like the story of Moses who wanted to encounter the living God. God said that no one has seen the face of God and lived, so Moses had to take cover in a cave (retreat into darkness) while the presence of God passed by (Exodus 33:12-23).

It's true that we cannot see the face of God and live (Exodus 33:20). At least the false self cannot live in the presence of God. As we draw nearer to God, we take cover in the dark while the false self is burned away. If we want to "see" (become aware) of the reality of God, the false self has to die, or let go of its dominance. For ultimately, as Father Richard rightly points out, everything belongs. It's just a matter of the false self dying to its prominence in one's life. This is the substance of the spiritual journey. This is what it means to do your inner work. Your false ideas, misperceptions, and skewed beliefs about God and, quite frankly, about yourselves have to metaphorically burn up in divine light.

One such season of darkness affected not only my spirit and mind, but my body too. It was autumn. I was giving an annual contemplative retreat. And it was there, when I was responsible for fifty people who had traveled from various places throughout the country, that I experienced the worst abdominal pain of my life. It completely took me out. Nothing I did provided relief. At the Benedictine Retreat Center about an hour away from Omaha, Nebraska, I was bent over with spasms and bloating and the most severe discomfort. I couldn't get comfortable no matter how I sat or laid. Because we were quite far from adequate health care and the night was fast approaching, I decided to suffer through the night in hopes that I could make it to the hospital in the city the next morning.

The following day, after several hours waiting in the emergency room and undergoing a series of tests, I learned I had a massive cyst on each of my ovaries, about the size of a tennis ball! The following days I was propelled into getting educated as fast as I could about women's reproductive health. (Hang in there, men!)

Long story short, endoscopic surgery was required to rule out cancer and confirm the diagnosis. Gratefully, after the procedure I learned there was definitely no cancer, but I did indeed have a serious disease— endometriosis. I had actually sustained quite a bit of emotional and community suffering the previous five years, and it seemed now my body was revealing the physical toll it had taken. I was faced with the challenge of healing my body. My faith was certainly tested during the trials I had endured with my community, and now it was tested yet again as I tried to find God in the mystery of physical pain and disease.

Early on after the diagnosis, I found myself on private retreat in the Cottonwood Mountains of Utah, diving deep into solitude, silence, and stillness.

Autumn was in full color in Utah, with the various trees turning from green to yellow, orange, and red. It was marvelous to behold such beauty each morning in those quiet hills. At the mountain peaks, winter had already set in.

Usually on retreat I spend most of my time in centering prayer. Alone, in nature, everything slows down. Even though I usually bring several books to read, I tend to read little. This time it was no different. Rest for body, mind, and soul was primary. It was no different except for one thing.

Because of the endometriosis, the first four days of the retreat my body was in need of tremendous rest. The symptoms of the disease can be excruciatingly painful, like a fifteen on a scale of one to ten. Some reports indicate the pain is more severe than childbirth. If you've ever had to endure heightened physical pain, you know that managing it affects not only the body but the mind and soul as well. I was discouraged. God seemed very distant, in fact absent.

And so there I was, on retreat, nursing and nourishing my wounded womb. Not exactly what I had planned, and yet, exactly what was needed.

Life often works like that. We have preconceived expectations for how circumstances in life will turn out: the kind of person we'll marry, the number of children we'll have, the kind of job in which we'll be employed. And sometimes, things don't turn out as we'd hoped. The marriage partner doesn't materialize; it's more difficult to get pregnant than imagined; the dream job doesn't work out. And yet, in our disappointment God can be found, nudging us awake, helping us realize that God knows what is needed for our ultimate fulfillment. Life gives us what is required for awakening and transformation. But do we have eyes to see and ears to hear?

There in Utah, I remembered a profound mystical experience in Bear Hermitage the previous year in the Sangre de Cristo Mountains of New Mexico. In those secluded hills, it dawned on me that I was in the womb of God. It was such an enlightening awareness that rooted me in deeper knowledge that nothing can separate me from God. God's got me. Though previous to this experience I had endured many months in the dark, not sensing God's presence, light broke through when I realized that I was being held in the womb of God. The womb is a quiet, hidden place. And the baby doesn't have knowledge of being held. The baby only enjoys the comfort of safety and provision. It is a wonder to wake up to the reality that we as adults are being held in God. This realization (beyond intellectual reflection but realized in my being) occurred a year before I was diagnosed with a disease that ironically affected my womb.

But a year later, in Utah, in solitude, silence, and stillness, I was suffering. I had no felt experience of being safely held in God. Where in the world was God?

I cried out in pain and discouragement and I sat. I heard nothing. I felt alone. And I could do very little but attempt to rest in meditation. Then suddenly, in the quietness, I realized, to my utter amazement, that *God* is in *my* womb. A year earlier it was the awareness that I am in God. But here in Utah the realization was reversed: *God* is in *me*. God is in the diseased parts of our bodies as well as the healthy parts. God is in my suffering and in yours. There's absolutely nothing that can separate us from God (Psalm 139).

Both are true at the same time: we are in God and God is in us. But it takes experiences of darkness and God's felt absence to awaken to this.

As we rest more deeply in God, God can rest more deeply in us. This is the way of divine union. And as our consciousness stabilizes in this union, we can cooperate with God in the healing of our world. Unitive consciousness is for each of us. How we express that oneness is unique.

There, in the snowy surroundings of Utah, it dawned on me that something mystical was started in the snowy "Blood of Christ" mountains of New Mexico a year earlier. Now, as I endured physical pain and spiritual darkness, I was realizing and embodying that mystery. It was as if I was undergoing a spiritual blood transfusion. There is always meaning to be found in our suffering. The following poem captures the light at work in me when all grew dim.

> Remember when You hemmed me in
> And we were alone
> You and I
> You helped me make my home in You
> In your womb
> There in the "Blood of Christ" Mountains
>
> * * *
>
> And your blood began to circulate
> And discovered it could not freely flow
> You whispered ever so gently,
> "What is hindering must go."

Resistances to God's presence. Obstacles to love. Fear, anger, unforgiveness. These kinds of things hinder the divine from flowing in and through us. When we are serious about the spiritual journey, we will traverse all manner of inner landscapes in an effort to overcome barriers and relinquish opposition.

On the contemplative path, darkness is indeed light. Father Richard says, "God is Light, yet this full light is hidden in darkness (John 1:5) so only the sincere seeker finds it."[1]

God may *feel* absent. We may *feel* alone. But all the while, God's presence is a burning flame, healing us and freeing us, and expanding our field of awareness. When the work of grace for that season is complete, we emerge with greater perception to sense and know God. We are a little bit more aligned, a little bit more at one.

Darkness serves to position God less as the *object* of awareness and more as the *subject* of existence. You could say

DARKNESS SERVES TO POSITION GOD LESS AS THE *OBJECT* OF AWARENESS AND MORE AS THE *SUBJECT* OF EXISTENCE.

that darkness serves the process of "oneing"—that helpful description that Julian of Norwich has given us. She describes divine union like this:

> The soul is preciously knitted to God in its making, by a knot so subtle and so mighty that it is oned into God. In this oneing, it is made endlessly holy. Furthermore, God wants us to know that all the souls which are one day to be saved in heaven without end are knit in this same knot and oned in this oneing, and made holy in this one identical holiness.[2]

Julian continues,

> By myself I am nothing at all, but in general, I am in the oneing of love. For it is in this oneing that the life of all people exists.[3]

> In the sight of God all persons are oned, and one person is all people.[4]

> The love of God creates in us such a *oneing* that when it is truly seen, no one can separate themselves from another.[5]

> In the sight of God all humans are oned, and one person is all people and all people are in one person.[6]

When we learn to walk in the dark, we wake up to the reality that we are knitted into an unbreakable knot of connection with God and the human family.

Christian mysticism is about encountering Mystery in such a way that we are changed—quite literally—heart, mind, and body. Obscurity serves to take us deeper into trust and faith where the sickness that hinders greater awareness of our union with God and one another can be cured. But it is so difficult to find our way through darkness. Thankfully, we can turn to the sages, and no teacher in the Christian tradition is wiser about the role of darkness than John of the Cross.

A COMPANION THROUGH THE DARK

Years ago, after that initial crisis of faith, during a long spiritually dark night, I met John of the Cross. Not in person, of course, but through his enduring spiritual classic, *Dark Night of the Soul*. John of the Cross, disciple of the elder Teresa of Ávila, was a sixteenth-century Discalced Carmelite mystic, priest, and poet. He lived through incredible hardship and persecution at the hands of his fellow monks, and it was through his suffering that he emerged one of the greatest spiritual directors in the Christian tradition.

During a time when I felt particularly alone, John of the Cross was a comforting companion. Like no one else in my life, this beloved teacher was able to encourage and guide me through the murky waters of the spiritual journey. In his world-renowned, evocative poem, *Dark Night of the Soul*, he illuminates the irony that when we are experiencing spiritual darkness, we are actually encountering divine light, a light of love that consumes us.

> It is well to observe at this point that this purgative and loving knowledge or Divine light whereof we here speak acts upon the soul which it is purging and preparing for perfect union with it in the same way as fire acts upon a log of wood in order to transform it into itself; for material fire, acting upon wood, first of all begins to dry it, by driving out its moisture and causing it to shed the water which it contains within itself. Then it begins to make it black, dark and unsightly, and even to give forth a bad odour, and, as it dries it little by little, it brings out and drives away all the dark and unsightly accidents which are contrary to the nature of fire. And, finally, it begins to kindle it externally and give it heat, and at the last transforms it into itself and makes it as beautiful as fire.[7]

In our age of information overload, postmodern people are overwhelmed with life. We work too much, overindulge in digital stimulation, smother our schedules, and worry about every little thing. We are perpetually fragmented, distracted, and disconnected from our centermost being where God dwells. We are desperate for prayer that helps us practice being alone, being quiet, and being still. In this context, the mysticism of John of the Cross has never been more relevant than it is today.

John of the Cross was an outstanding friar of sixteenth-century Spain, short in stature but great in spiritual wisdom. He was born in 1542 in Fontiveros, Spain, near Àvila, to a poor converso family. Conversos were descendants of Jewish converts to Christianity. He died at just forty-nine years of age in Ubeda, Spain, in 1591.

John belonged to the Carmelite order at a time when it was infected with a lot of corruption—much like the institutional church of its time. Teresa of Àvila, his elder, was an avid reformer, and John was completely devoted to her. John met Teresa when she was fifty-two and he was just twenty-five. He quickly became her disciple and partner in reforming the Carmelite order. Together, despite great opposition, they managed to establish the Discalced (shoeless) Carmelites in the spirit of the desert mothers and fathers. They reformed the order to apply the vows of poverty, chastity, and obedience with greater zeal and inspired the wider church to apply the radical teachings of Jesus to their life. Both John and Teresa are revered today as "Doctors of the Church"—a title given by the Catholic Church to saints who hold particular depth of insight and wisdom that is relevant in any age.

Along the way, some of the Carmelites, opposed to reform, took John captive. He was secretly abducted by night from Àvila and taken to a monastery in Toledo, where he was imprisoned under very severe conditions for nine months before he escaped. His captors subjected him to the harshest conditions: he was whipped weekly before his religious brothers and kept in strict isolation in a ten- by six-foot cell with little to no light. He was given no change of clothing and a meager diet of water, bread, and scraps of fish. During this time, he managed to compose a great portion of *Spiritual Canticle* and likely composed parts of his famous poem *Dark Night of the Soul*—which spiritual seekers tend to stumble on when they need it most. Volumes of books have been written about *Dark Night of the Soul*, trying to help people glean its wisdom.

John's name unashamedly reveals the antidote for our soul's sickness: the cross.[8] His path is not for the faint of heart; it requires courage and devotion. Essentially, his way is that of following Jesus, dying to self or emptying self to make room for the all-consuming presence of God (Philippians 2).

Though his mysticism offers ultimate fulfillment, it is not for everyone. John says his way is the quickest route to living in the source of love, our Creator, our God. But he also says that not all are called to this particular path.[9] Still, John's spirituality is an invitation of prayer for spiritual pilgrims looking for personal transformation to impact a world in need of love.

PRAYER FOR DEVOTED SEEKERS

John's predominant reader or disciple is someone dedicated to a life of *kataphatic* prayer and discursive meditation—which is virtually the only kind of prayer Western Christianity has taught us. This type of prayer utilizes concepts and images to relate to God.

It's true that John is also writing to those who have given themselves to the vowed religious life, with many more hours in the day given to such prayer than most of us are afforded. He speaks of a natural progression the prayerful person may come to in prayer— when the usual practices run dry and one finds it difficult, if not impossible, to pray with the faculties (reason, imagination, feelings, and will). Essentially, at this point, one progresses instinctively into *apophatic* prayer—prayer of quiet, without concepts and images. We'll explore more of this topic in chapter seven.

In the West, thanks to modern contemplative teachers and mystics like Basil Pennington, Thomas Keating, Richard Rohr, Cynthia Bourgeault, Tilden Edwards, and Laurence Freeman, now the average layperson, in addition to the vowed nun or monk, has access to an apophatic prayer method that conditions one for John's teaching. In this kind of prayer, one of nakedness and poverty, as John calls it, we are made more and more open or receptive to God's action in our soul and, consequently, in our life.[10]

John's mysticism invites us to empty our self so that God can have more space to live more fully within and through us. This is the way of the Paschal mystery. As we let go of control and yield to God in contemplative prayer, we will undergo the way of Jesus—suffering, death, and ultimately resurrected life. As the old adage goes, "No pain, no gain." The natural order in all of life is death and rebirth. If we want to live an abundant life, we will gladly yield to this process. For like John discovered, the way of the cross is our ultimate peace and fulfillment.

PERSONAL TRANSFORMATION FOR A WORLD IN NEED OF LOVE

The Christian contemplative path is traditionally marked by the spiritual dynamics of purgation, illumination, and union. In the process of transformation, we journey through these states or ways.

Purgation is the juncture primarily at the beginning of the spiritual journey when our disordered attachments are exposed and our self-serving tendencies are purified. It usually comes by way of suffering or temptation or both. The lowly attachments that we've had toward gratifying our false self are purged or burned up in the light of God, so to speak. During this stage, we are being drawn to desire the will of God more in every area of our life. Yet, we still act out of our disordered attachments, doing what *we* (false self) will rather than being aligned with *God's* will and our truest self.

Illumination involves less attachment to gratifying the desires of the false self, increased desire for the will of God, and greater spiritual insights, revelations, and consolations. During this stage, we are less likely to intentionally do harmful things to others, but unconscious compulsions of thought or unconscious disordered motivations are likely still at work. This stage may last a very long time as God purifies us at ever deepening levels of our psyche and being. And while consolations are at play, desolations are too. In fact, we may experience intense spiritual suffering as circumstances of life or prayer create conditions in which we feel as if we are dying. The false self-identity we have clung to for so long is passing away to make room for the resurrected true self-identity as the beloved of God. John teaches that though this process is arduous; it is also enlightening. And the touches of God along the way make it possible for us to stay on this rigorous path of transformation.[11]

Union is the obvious stage of *at-one-ment* with God. In other religious traditions it might be similar to *enlightenment*. At this stage, one has endured enough purification of the false self that one is abiding continuously, or almost continuously, in God-awareness. People at this stage are no longer attached to gratifying the self and instead are disposed to be of service to God and others. Their lives are marked by fecund acts of loving, selfless service.

With the help of table 1, the Jesuit Richard Hauser describes well this classic Christian path of growth and transformation in his book *Becoming a Contemplative in Action*.[12] The first column outlines the particular stage in the journey. The second column indicates how one relates to Christ in the process of conversion. And the third column distinguishes the quality of prayer generally experienced at each stage. It's important to keep in mind, however, that this is not a linear journey. It's more of a labyrinth. We move through it by grace, in and out of center, in a progression of greater awakening and union.

Table 1. The Christian Spiritual Path

STAGE OF THE JOURNEY	FOCUS OF DAILY LIVING	QUALITY OF PRAYER
Unawakened Self	Law and commandments	Vocal
(Relationship to Christ by fidelity to obligations)		
AWAKENING OF THE SELF TO THE SPIRIT (Relationship to Christ by fidelity to the Spirit)		
Purgative Way	Imitation of Christ: Patterns of action Continuing conversion: Temptations • Fluctuations of heart • Fluctuations of action	Talking to the Lord Mind active Meditation
Illuminative Way	Imitation of Christ: Quality of heart Continuing conversion: Temptations • Fluctuation of heart • *No* fluctuation of action	Being with the Lord Mind attentive: I-Thou Beginning contemplation
Unitive Way	Imitation of Christ: Zeal for service Continuing conversion: Temptations • *No* fluctuations of heart • *No* fluctuation of action	Being one in the Lord Mind absorbed in the Lord Advanced contemplation

John teaches that the process of purgation and illumination in our journey toward union with God is gradual.[13] And there are degrees of union.[14] Yes, there will be experiences of purification of our senses that are painful, because we desire to gratify the passions of what tradition calls the capital sins: pride, greed, lust, anger, gluttony, envy, and sloth. It is not easy at first to deny these attachments, or "appetites," as John calls them. But the result of this painful passage is indescribable joy.[15] Our lowly attachments pale in comparison to the gifts and graces of increased awareness of the divine.

The process of unification necessarily involves darkness. And John wisely uncovers two distinguishing nights in the dark night of the soul experience: the *night of sense* and the *night of spirit*. The night of sense seems to occur when one transitions from purgative (purification) to illuminative (enlightening). The night of spirit seems to take place when one transitions from illuminative to unitive (oneness with God). But remember, this journey is not linear. We may move in and out of the night of sense for many years before we ever experience a night of spirit. Likewise, it may take many nights of spirit before complete oneness is realized.

First, let us consider the night of sense. Over time, through contemplative prayer, as we rest in God in faith, a deep interior work takes place in our unconsciousness. Layer after layer of defenses against dwelling in the love of God gets removed, beginning with the surfacemost part of us—our senses. This season of darkness is distinguished by God purposefully withdrawing consolations—those warm, fuzzy feelings or "senses" and reassurances of God's presence. This can be very troubling for seekers, thinking that they have done something to cause God to withdraw from them. But instead, this is the necessary process by which one's lingering internal barriers to the divine are exposed. One learns during this stage to pursue the *God of consolations* rather than the *consolations of God*.

The process of transformation is not something we can do for ourselves. It is truly the work of God in us. During the night of sense, we walk in blind faith and trust that God is doing a hidden work in us. We relinquish control. We are led through the shadows. We can only choose to yield or not yield to this secret work. As John teaches, we *can* indeed choose to consent or reject the divine action of God within us.[16] The practice of contemplative prayer helps us say yes when our disordered attachments and psychological resistances scream, "No!"

With God's grace, we yield to this loving liberation in darkness of faith. We can't see with our sight what is happening in us, and we don't know with our intellect what's going on within. Instead, through contemplative prayer, we learn to let go of control in all manner of our senses. Accordingly, the fruit of this kind of prayer is evidenced in the active life, not in the prayer itself. John says the benefits of the dark night of sense are growth in self-knowledge and knowledge of God, communion with God in all of life, clarity, humility, and love of others.[17]

This process of being led through the dark is so utterly liberating. We are freed of self-centeredness and self-absorption, and emancipated into love. This is indeed a process, and remember that there are degrees of union. John writes, "The more degrees of love it has, the more deeply it enters into God and centers itself in Him."[18] As we taste more and more of this emancipation and love, we become increasingly aligned with the ways of God.[19] This makes us receptive for the night of spirit. The night of sense is the *surface* project. The night of spirit aims at the *root* of our compulsions and disordered attachments that hold us in captivity. This is the hidden inner work of Spirit that Father Thomas calls "divine therapy."

Once we are sufficiently weaned from dependence on our senses, we may experience a night of spirit. The night of spirit can be even more excruciating than the night of sense because it brings one into a death of self. But it can also be very gradual over time as one commits to regular meditation.

In the night of sense, John says the log of wood (soul) is *blackened* during the burning process of fire. In the night of spirit, the log of wood (soul) is *consumed*. Remember, contemplative spirituality is much more than wellness. Its radical objective is the destruction of the separate self.

During a visit with Father Thomas very late in his life, when asked how he was doing, he responded, "Well, I'm busy dying." When asked what that is like, he responded, "Well, it's becoming . . . nothing." In that conversation, he mentioned how he was suffering. And it seemed to me that he was enduring this very passage through the night of spirit, a log of wood being completely consumed by God. To be in his presence at that time was like being in the presence of a burning log, the flames of God burning brightly. We were transfixed on his every word, and each utterance warmed our soul in the precise way that each of us needed.

With every degree of this profound transformation through darkness, we are resurrected more and more into the life of Christ. And

> WITH EVERY
> DEGREE OF THIS
> PROFOUND
> TRANSFORMATION
> THROUGH
> DARKNESS, WE
> ARE RESURRECTED
> MORE AND MORE
> INTO THE LIFE
> OF CHRIST.

Jesus promised that we would do even greater things than he (John 14:12). This is the possibility, if we take the spiritual journey or the way of the cross seriously.

Gradually, through the mysterious season of darkness, God excavates our interior landscape, uprooting the layers of imperfections that keep us from fully cooperating with God in our world. Our deeply embedded illusions about our self, God, and others orient us toward psychological, behavioral, and spiritual compulsion, addiction, and general unhappiness. Our unhappiness is our imperfection or sickness. To protect the vulnerable root of our disease we unconsciously build up fortifications, defenses to God's healing presence. Eventually, as we stay faithful to the dark night of prayer, God will uncover the root of our sickness. There a wound of separation from God and others is exposed that can now receive healing. Finally, our defenses are dismantled and the burning flame of God's love breaks through our consciousness.[20] We realize we are in God and God is in us.

Over time, as we let go into God, our entire being is illuminated. We begin to see with a long and broad view; we grow in oneness with the whole created world; we love more freely and generously. We become vessels in which Christ can pour out his energy, his love, and his healing to a world that desperately needs it.[21]

The contemplative prayer that John expounds on is an invitation to rest, to be, and to let God be God in our life. Over time as we open ourselves to this secret work of Spirit, our overcrowded life relents to solitude, noise gives way to silence, and restlessness transforms to stillness—both interiorly in our soul and exteriorly in our life and vocation. This work of grace makes it possible to *respond* to life circumstances rather than *react*. Once we taste divine peace and love within, we are liberated to share such graces with others.

Peace and love cannot come to our world until we have uncovered them from within. And true virtues of this nature come from abiding in the Source of such bountiful goodness.[22] John puts it this way: "Happy is the life and state, and happy the person who attains it, where everything is now the substance of love."[23] From this pure connection with God flows an abundance of love to heal the world. This is what Jesus demonstrated in his life, death, and resurrection, what John of the Cross testifies to, and what we too can experience by the merciful grace of our Creator.

Practice: Lectio Divina

Lectio divina, which means "divine reading" or "sacred reading," is an ancient practice of praying Holy Scripture. *Lectio divina* helps us open to divine love through the process of purgation, illumination, and union. Over time, we become more aware of being in God and God being in us. In the first few stages of this practice we utilize the senses. In the final stage, we let go of our senses and rest in faith. The steps move us naturally from acquaintance with the divine, to friendship, to union.

One of the oldest monastic forms of prayer, *lectio divina* can be traced back to the fourth- and fifth-century desert mothers and fathers. Later, it was incorporated into Saint Benedict's monastic rule of life. Today, this practice is still very common in monasteries.

During *lectio divina*, the practitioner listens with the heart to the sacred text for what they hear being said to them through the text. The method of *lectio divina* includes four phases: reading (*lectio*), reflecting on (*meditatio*), responding to (*oratio*), and resting in (*contemplatio*), with the aim of nourishing and deepening one's relationship with God.

With experience, this practice becomes a dynamic flow, rather than a strictly linear process. Within the flow, we learn to yield more and more to God's love. In the beginning, it may be helpful to be very conscious of all four phases. But in time, one flows through the stages effortlessly, finally resting in *contemplatio*.

You may use this method of prayer for any text you hold sacred. Many find the parables of Jesus or the psalms of David to be accessible texts for this practice. The following steps will guide you.

1. Take a few deep breaths and let yourself grow aware of the present moment. Acknowledge the presence of the Holy Spirit.
2. During the first reading of the text you've chosen, take in all the sights, sounds, and textures of the text (*lectio*).
3. During the second reading, listen for a word or phrase that stands out to you (*meditatio*).
4. Read the text a third time, and share your heartfelt response to God (*oratio*).
5. During the final reading, rest in your experience with the sacred text (*contemplatio*).

For more information visit https://gravitycenter.com /practice/lectio-divina/.

CHAPTER FIVE

EXPLORING A DEEP WELL

From their innermost being will
flow rivers of living water.

JOHN 7:38

Place your mind before the mirror of eternity!
Place your soul in the brilliance of glory! And
transform your entire being into the image
of the Godhead Itself through contemplation.

ST. CLARE OF ASSISI

DID YOU EVER MEET someone and come to a quick negative judgment about who they were? Then, after spending time with the person, being really present to them, you realized they weren't at all who you thought they were? Actually, you realized the person had wonderful qualities that you admired?

It's easy to cruise through interactions with others without really being present, and thus miss so many of the gifts they offer.

We do this to our self too. Eager to move through life, often we aren't present, we have misperceptions about who we are, and we neglect the full potential of our personhood. It's only when our identity is firmly established that we can bring that self to bear on the world. Like Odysseus in Homer's epic *Odyssey*, we must set out on a journey to discover who we are. Once we find our true self, we uncover the courage to metaphorically return home. Setting off on the adventure is an enduring exploration for truth. This is how all great shero and hero stories begin.

Part of the disillusionment with Christianity today is the shallowness of its teaching. Sam Pascoe, an American scholar, is widely quoted as saying: "Christianity started out in Palestine as a fellowship; it moved to Greece and became a philosophy; it moved to Italy and became an institution; it moved to Europe and became a culture; it came to America and became an enterprise."[1] Western Christianity was taken to the marketplace years ago. Consequently, much of the teaching offered in the church has been watered down for easy consumption. A palatable prescription for belief is too often rendered instead of guidance and support for the struggle of living into our potential as children of God. Many people find church services wanting, the worship music and teaching to be shallow, not relating to our complex human condition and our soul's voyage.

Contemplative Christianity assumes the depths of the high seas. It rises from the deep well of presence, perception, and personhood. When nurtured, the contemplative dimension of our faith overflows into streams of living water for others (John 4:14; 7:38). But one must be relatively self-actualized to be ready for the depths from which contemplative spirituality comes. What is more, it generally takes a considerable amount of chronological time and life experience to establish a strong sense of self in the world.

Let me be clear. The self is not an inherently bad entity. It just is. It's a necessary part of being human and the fundamental starting point for the spiritual journey.

First, we *grow up*.[2] Our family of origin gives us context and a container for who we are and for what we're capable of.[3] If our family is relatively healthy, we are fortunate to be more or less prepared to mature into adulthood. But if our family is dysfunctional (which is more often the case), then we will likely have a number of challenges threatening the process of growing up and developing a confident sense of self. Sometimes mentors emerge to help fill in the gaps for nurturing what was neglected. Other times counseling and psychotherapy offer the support needed. Whatever it takes to grow up, one way or another life will usually present us with opportunities to self-actualize.

But once that self is established, the onward voyage begins. We set out into the great wide world to prove our self or attempt to make a difference. And inevitably, we experience a rude awakening. Experience reveals that we are not who we thought we were. All those years of crafting a container or a sense of self seem futile. The self we created is not true, not real. We have built our house on sand. We have manufactured a personality, a mask, a poor resemblance of our essence and true nature.

At this point we have a choice. Either we can ignore the signs pointing toward liberation from our personality, or we can plumb the depths and let experience be our teacher. If we choose the latter, it is time to *clean up*—to clean up the lies we've listened to about who we are and the happiness programs we've bought into.

At this juncture in the journey, contemplative spirituality is absolutely crucial. We need teaching that provides a road map for what's ahead, and we need practices that can support us to stay on the path of liberation. It's far too easy to go back to sleep under the familiar comfort of our mask, with its illusions that reinforce the false self. But the Christian path involves dismantling our false identity. Jesus put it this way: "You who have found your life will lose it, and you who lose your life for my sake will find it" (Matthew 10:39).

And so, the spiritual journey begins. And it begins with *presence*. Presence is the capacity to be right here, right now. Contemplation is all about being present. I never understood this more than when Basil came into my life.

Chris and I don't have children. Eight years into our marriage we determined to forgo birthing our own so that we could be more available to the children we'd come to know and love around the world. By the time of our twentieth wedding anniversary, most all of those children had grown up. And somewhat like empty-nesters, we found ourselves more alone. Life was slowing down a little for me. I wasn't traveling as much as I used to. And to my surprise, I found myself desiring to adopt a dog.

Keep in mind, in all our years of life together, the only pet we'd ever owned was a beta fish. And believe it or not, one year we actually put that fish in a Nalgene water bottle (filled with water, of course) and travelled throughout Asia with him. We have the photos to prove it. A beta fish was the extent of our capacity in those years to be responsible for an additional member of our nuclear family. Adopting a dog would be a much larger commitment—one Chris wasn't sure we were ready for.

I blame Rudy for planting the desire for Basil. Rudy is a medium-sized, long-haired, reddish-brown rescue dog. At just three years of age he was found fending for himself on the streets of Philadelphia. We met him while visiting his humans, Phil and Sandi, in Marco Island, Florida. Our first morning, Rudy eagerly ventured into our room, jumped up on our bed (which we found out later he was normally forbidden to do), and enthusiastically welcomed us into a new day. We were smitten. That day, I began riddling Phil with questions about Rudy. How long have you had him? Where did you find him? How did you find him? How did you train him?—he was so well behaved. And thus my world expanded into the realms of pet rescue, the Pet Finder website, and the unique personalities of dogs.

Now it's important you understand that Chris and I were not "dog people." When meeting the occasional domestic dog, we really rarely gave them a second thought. After all the years spending time with children in poverty, we really hadn't found much of an appreciation for pets beyond the low-maintenance beta fish. But Rudy was different. Or perhaps *we* were different at that point. I think Rudy sensed we had a dog-shaped hole in our heart that needed to be filled.

Not long after leaving Marco Island, I brought up the idea of adopting a dog to Chris, and he generously entertained the thought. I didn't realize at the time that he hadn't taken me seriously. Nearly a year passed, and my desire to adopt a dog only intensified. I had spent many months stalking online images of orphaned puppies at pet rescues and searching for "the one." I didn't know for sure what kind of dog I wanted, but friends told me not to worry, that I would know when I found her or him.

One evening I sat Chris down and let him know that it was important to me that he be as committed to the decision as I was. I knew I didn't want to be an unsupported single dog parent. I needed to know he would help assume responsibility. He understood, and that night we agreed to a small, brown, female dog.

Later that summer Chris was in Cambodia for work. While there, a friend remarked about one of my Facebook posts. "So, I hear you're getting a dog." Chris responded, "Yeah, that will never happen."

Meanwhile, I continued to search.

A few short months later, Chris was in Canada for work. (Yes, that guy keeps a mean travel schedule. If we ever adopted a dog I knew I'd have to be the primary caregiver.) It was a Friday evening and I drove to the opposite side of town for a puppy "meet and greet." While there, I met a few dogs, but none of them seemed to be the one. Mary Anne was the volunteer working that evening. I visited with her for a while and explained to her how green I was at searching for a puppy. I told her how I had been looking for nearly a year and had yet to find the right one. She listened intently to my story as I shared about the life that Chris and I live. She then encouraged me to look through their booklet of photos of all the dogs available for adoption that were not present that evening. Immediately, I was drawn to one. When I pointed to his photo, Mary Anne's eyes lit up. She exclaimed, "Oh he's amazing! He would be perfect for you! I know his foster mom. I'll call her right now." The next thing I knew I was making arrangements to meet this little five-month-old puppy.

The following day, I ventured out to the same location where a bigger "meet and greet" was happening than the night before. I met several dogs and held a few, but none of them seemed to be the one. Then Stephanie, the foster mom, arrived with the cutest little brown dog I'd ever seen in my entire life. He was so small, with big inviting eyes, and seemed quite vulnerable. He was clearly overwhelmed with all the people and animals. But instantly we made a connection. The only problem was that Chris and I had agreed to a *small*, brown, *female* dog. This one was *male* and likely would be *medium-sized*.

Since Chris was out of town, I didn't feel comfortable adopting the puppy right then and there. So I asked Stephanie if we could wait to make a decision in a few days after my husband returned. She agreed.

Then out of the corner of my eye I saw that another couple was eyeing the puppy; they quickly began inquiring. My heart sank. What if they end up adopting him? I began to panic. It was then I realized he was *the one*.

I quickly sent a photo of the little guy to Chris, concerned that he would not be persuaded because the puppy didn't fit our agreed upon criteria. Moments later, to my surprise, he responded, "Aww. That's a cute puppy!"

My heart leapt.

I'm not exaggerating when I say this little dog was the most adorable I had ever seen. So, I posted a photo on Chris' Facebook wall to garner public support. Unbeknownst to Chris, who was facilitating an Enneagram workshop that afternoon, hundreds of comments were made encouraging him to welcome this puppy into our family.

I swiftly put into motion everything I could to arrange a meeting for Chris and the dog. Later that evening I spoke with Stephanie. She said that the couple I saw did indeed want to adopt him, but that she and Mary Anne had a special feeling about Chris and me. She felt the puppy was meant for us. So she agreed to put the other couple on hold until Chris could meet him.

A few days later, the big day came. Stephanie brought the puppy to our home, and to my gladness, he remembered me. He greeted me warmly and began to settle in. Chris had been upstairs and when he descended, the sweet little dog got directly in front of me and warned Chris with his innocent bark not to come any nearer. He had taken up a protective stance for me already. Chris knew in that moment that he was meant to be ours. Soon the puppy understood that Chris was not a threat but a crucial part of the pack. He was then delighted for Chris to give him a tour of the home. They've been bonded ever since.

My puppy, Basil, teaches me to be present. He's older and bigger now than he was when he first joined our family, but he'll always be our "puppy." When Basil and I are together, time stands still. And he has such a way of getting my attention. At home in the evenings if I've been too busy on my phone or computer, he will paw at me and some-times cry and demand that I look at him. Then he makes me lie down so he can curl up all forty pounds of himself and plop directly on my tummy. Basil makes me be with him in the moment. Nothing else matters at those times but our connection.

Chris says we wanted a small, brown, female dog, but ended up with a honey-bourbon, gender-fluid, extra medium dog. If we're pre-sent, we discover that exactly what we need is waiting for us. It may not be what we expected, but it proves to be better than we could have imagined.

I used to regularly travel the world. Every eighteen months I would jet-set from Middle America to various countries across the globe. Any given year I would be on forty to fifty flight segments. But now I don't want to leave my dog. Basil helps me slow down and be present. When Basil wants to go out to play, he's in the moment. When Basil wants a drink of water, he's in the moment. When he wants to play or eat or cuddle, he helps me get out of my head and into the present. He reminds me to be right here, right now because now is all he has, and I'm all he's got. Basil doesn't dwell on the past or fret about the future. He lives in the now and he helps me do the same. He forces me to be present to him, who is always present to the moment he's in.

When we establish presence, we choose to be in the now. But our mind has a terrible time being present. It is very busy ruminating on the past or worrying about the future. Spiritual awakening and growth cannot arise from the past or the future but only the present. Stabilizing presence of mind is the first step toward transformation. But the mind is like a boat tossed this way and that in the sea (Ephesians 4:14; James 1:6). So, we are desperate for practices that train the lower mind to calm down. Once the lower mind calms down, we can gain access to our higher mind, or what Paul calls "the mind of Christ" (1 Corinthians 2:11-16; Philippians 2:5-11). This is exactly what contemplative prayer helps us do.

Presence of mind and heart is the doorway into divine presence. Presence is intimate and vulnerable, thus it requires a certain degree of maturity. The more present we are, the more capable we are of searching the depths of self, truth, and meaning. Once established in the present moment, we are poised to wake up, open our eyes, and begin to see or perceive more clearly. *Perception* is the next critical component to contemplative spirituality. Perception is *how* we see.

I've always found it interesting that so much of Jesus' ministry focused on recovering sight for those who were blind. Having the eyes to see reality, the ears to hear truth, and the mind to integrate both is what contemplative spirituality is all about. All the great spiritual teachers agree, much of this life is about removing the blinders, dismantling illusions, and having eyes to see (Isaiah 6:10; Jeremiah 5:21; Ezekiel 12:2; Matthew 13:15; Mark 8:17-18).

Clear perception allows us to realize that we are beloved children of God, that there's nothing we can do to earn or lose that identity. This kind of perception helps us realize that I am not defined by what I do, what I say, or what others think of me. I am beloved, a child of God with divine DNA.

Furthermore, it's right perception that enabled Jesus to pray while being crucified, "Father forgive them. They don't know what they're doing." Right perception allows us to see through hatred and violence into the woundedness and pain of the one wreaking havoc. Without proper perception, we too easily meet anger with anger, violence with violence, hate with hate. Something has to break this cycle for peace to be established. Contemplative practice interrupts the madness. Presence and perception help birth peace.

Presence and perception then lead us into establishing a liberated *personhood*. Personhood is different from personality. Personality is our best attempt to form an identity as a separate self. "Me against the world." As we progress on the spiritual journey, it's not as if we lose our identity. The self remains. Only, in the spiritual life, the self that was once formed as a separate identity now awakens into dynamic unity with God and solidarity with others. This is personhood: a person who is an individual united with all reality—an eye within the body (1 Corinthians 12).

Many Christians today are frustrated and disillusioned with their local church experience because they find the emphasis on orthodoxy fails to address their most impeding obstacles to developing personhood. Ascribing to "right belief" isn't helping with the everyday challenges of discerning purpose, being faithful in vocation, accessing patience, mercy, and long-suffering in relationship, and loving and forgiving those who hurt us. We are thirsty people, looking for water that satiates from the well that never runs dry (John 4). Contemplative practice draws forth living water from the well deep within (Luke 17:21).

> CONTEMPLATIVE PRACTICE DRAWS FORTH LIVING WATER FROM THE WELL DEEP WITHIN.

PRESENCE OF MIND, PRESENCE OF BEING

The crisis of faith I experienced after visiting war-torn Freetown, Sierra Leone, was a rude awakening. Previously, in all my years of social justice work and trying to set the world right, I had met the pain and suffering of the world with my ability to do something about it. Suffering was a problem to be solved. And someone was responsible. The problem, as I saw it, was greed and inequality. So, with my personality intact, I set out in the world to motivate people to be more generous, not only with their money but with their lifestyle and service too.

In the face of the complexities of war and subsequent contradictions and paradoxes that could not be problem-solved, my personality with its modus operandi collapsed. I no longer had the answers to the misery of my new friends. And therefore, I began to question everything. I was at a crossroads. Either I could ignore the signs pointing to the liberation of my essence (true self) from the prison of my personality (false self), or I could embark on an exploration into the depths of self. I had lived a very harried life, traveling from one humanitarian crisis to another. The antidote to my sickness was *presence*. It was time to cultivate the capacity to be right here, right now. Stop running. Stop hiding. Stop doing. Learn to be.

STOP RUNNING.
STOP HIDING.
STOP DOING.
LEARN TO BE.

Contradictions and paradoxes have a way of bringing us to our knees. Through failure or suffering we are confronted with the limits of our personality and its coping mechanisms. It can be difficult to continue on. At times like these we need wise teachers to remind us that this may feel like an end, but it's also an important beginning. It's the beginning of waking up into freedom from personality and the limitations of our happiness programs.

Presence of mind and presence of being became essential for accessing an interior stable center while the structure of my personality, worldview, and theology crumbled. Contemplative prayer offered a way for me to be with the pain and confusion of the psychological deconstruction I experienced. Over time, presence—being right here, right now—became more established. I learned to recognize the ways my personality was tempted to run or hide. Presence helped me resist that temptation and instead be with reality, even suffering. To be with reality required the determination to stare it in the face and embrace it (when everything in me wanted to resist it). In doing so, my true nature, my true identity, began to emerge from behind the mask. With such interior stabilization in place, perception began to clarify.

It was a small child I once knew from West Bengal who first helped sharpen my sight.

It was a dark and rainy night in Kolkata, India. Our staff and friends had gathered for a traditional Indian meal. We were all sitting around visiting while we waited for the food to be served. One friend got out his guitar and started playing to pass the time. And then a little boy walked in.

Safi. Just a child, no older than ten. Born to an impoverished mother and father, Safi grew up in an orphanage. Just recently he'd been adopted by a family in the United States.

This young, dynamic boy was a friend of our community, and so he had been invited to share one last meal with a group of people who loved him so dearly.

As we spent time together, I learned that Safi loves music. As our friend played the guitar, Safi went straight to him, put his ear down close to the instrument, and started strumming along. It was astonishing to watch Safi play so naturally.

You see, Safi is blind.

Later that evening, with full, satisfied bellies and gratitude in our hearts, we sat on the floor in a circle to pray. Safi called out, "Where's Chris?" He was very interested in knowing where my husband was.

Chris answered, "Over here." And Safi walked directly to him, put his hand on Chris's shoulder and stood with a confidence that rivals a statesman.

Chris looked up at Safi and asked, "What should we pray for? What do you want?" And without missing a beat, Safi said, "I want to see."

In the warm, candlelit room, we all tried to hold back the tears as we witnessed this child's bold faith. The prayer meeting ensued, and Safi cried out, "Jesus, give me the eyes!"

Safi was born physically blind. But until we embark on the spiritual journey, we are all spiritually blind. We are struggling to see God, let alone follow Jesus. It's when we are ready for bold faith and transformational freedom that we identify with Safi and the blind man on the road to Jericho who cried out, "Jesus, Son of David, have mercy on me!" (Luke 18:38).

And how does Jesus respond?

"What can I do for you?"

You see, Jesus never imposes. Always a gentleman, he asks how he can be of help. And in his generous restraint, he gives us the opportunity to recognize our human condition, tap into our deepest desires, and ask for his touch. That kind of self-awareness is the key to liberation.

When we establish presence, we naturally begin to see reality more clearly, and we are able to recognize the ways we are not yet free. Self-perception is the portal to grace—receiving from God what we cannot do for ourselves.

And so, with Safi and the blind man from the Gospels, we can courageously respond to Jesus' question: *I want to see! Jesus! Give me the eyes!*

Sharp self-perception then gives us the eyes to see the other—beyond the ways they act out and inflict hurt on the world. From there, personhood can emerge.

Contemplative prayer has over time given me the capacity for presence, so that pure perception is possible. With clarity, then, the real me is free to flow with the divine in co-creating the small segment of the world in which I inhabit.

Prior to this transformation, my personality, my sense of self, was operating primarily out of focus with God. I had manufactured a personality that was subject to what others thought about me, which severely limited my ability to say yes to the divine will. When I awoke to the structure of my personality, to my surprise, I realized that without it I don't actually cease to exist. Instead, removing the mask of my personality helped me uncover my core identity, my personhood, buried beneath the rubble of my deconstructed self. There *is* a self that is not tethered to personality, that—unlike the personality that is separate from God—has always existed *in* God. This is the self that lives and moves and has its being in God (Acts 17:28).

THE LESSER-KNOWN FRANCISCAN

During its formation, the international humanitarian community I was a part of found inspiration in the life of Francis of Assisi. I remember when I first learned of him. I mean, growing up I had seen the stone statues of a robed man with animals displayed in people's yards, but I don't remember ever hearing the story of Francis. Until one day, Chris showed me his San Damiano crucifix. He told me about this saint who lived with privilege and prosperity in the thirteenth century, who denied it all to give his life away for impoverished people. Saint Francis was the perfect icon for our missional community.

We too had grown up with relative privilege and prosperity compared to two-thirds of the world living in poverty. At that time, poverty-reduction organizations documented that 40,000 children were dying every day because they didn't have enough food to eat. We were mortified by that reality and knew that Jesus' way addressed such injustice.

I soon learned how, at the beginning of Francesco Bernardone's spiritual journey, he heard God's call to "rebuild the church." Often, he would climb down the hill from the town of Assisi to the Spoleto Valley to pray. Nestled in a wood of oak trees sat an old, abandoned church that had fallen into disrepair. It was there that Francis heard the mystical call from the San Damiano crucifix. Taking the message literally, he stole materials from his father's business to restore by hand the small church building. Only later did he realize the message to "rebuild the church" was pointing toward a much larger undertaking—reforming and purifying the people of God.

Francis's charism was all about becoming less so God could become more in and through his life. He lived radical poverty, identifying with the most vulnerable in his world. He quickly became our community's patron saint. Along with Jesus, Francis would help us find our way in a world of suffering and injustice.

Years later, after bearing witness to unspeakable human misery around the world, we had the opportunity to make pilgrimage to Assisi, Italy, the home of our icon. We were called there by something greater than ourselves. I was compelled to read whatever I could about the radical, barefoot saint.

During the long hours on the plane, during layovers in airports, and on the train from Rome to the little village of Assisi, I read and read. And then I met *her*. The lesser-known Franciscan who sometimes gets lost in Francis's shadow: Clare.

Like Francis, Clare possessed what we needed if we were going to stay committed to the spiritual journey and the task of healing our world. Francis had inspired us to be bold, radical, and self-giving. But it was Clare who unplugged the well of life-giving water in our souls.

Chris and I arrived in Assisi eager to visit all the sacred sights of these hallowed saints. The old, quaint Italian town rests in the province of Purugia in the Umbria region, on the western side of Monte Subasio. There it sits quietly on a hill, inhabited by just three thousand people. It is a small town with enormous influence. Some four to five million tourists visit each year. Its stone roads weave in and out of charming homes, bustling markets, delicious pizzerias, warm cafés, boutique wine shops, and historic churches. Assisi is truly remarkable. It seems the sky is bluer, the sun more radiant, and the air clearer.

We toured the magnificent Basilica di San Francesco, with its stunning frescoes and the sacred relics of Francis. We visited the Basilica di Santa Chiara, the final resting place of Clare. We saw the church where both Francis and Clare were baptized, and touched the humble cell where Francis died. We even found the place where Francis' father locked him in a cage and publicly humiliated him after Francis received clarity for his vocational calling. We ventured outside the city walls and found Francis's hermit cave. Eventually we made our way to the most sacred of all Assisi's sights, the humble Church of the San Damiano, with its crucifix that spoke to Francis. There we beheld the three olive trees that represent the Holy Trinity. Chris mischievously broke off a few of the holy branches, somehow got them through customs, and one of them now rests behind our replica of the San Damiano cross.

You may have noticed that a lot of the icons of Francis portray him communing with birds, sheep, donkeys, and even wolves. Legend describes Francis as being so holy the wild animals were unafraid of him; they would keep company with him. After visiting Assisi, Chris has a different take on all that.

As we walked up and down the hills between Assisi and the Spoleto Valley we got quite a workout. Those hills are steep. And it was no easy trek. Along the way, we were certain we spotted places where Francis would have prayed with the animals. Although Chris is convinced Francis's stops along the hillside were not so holy. Rather, he's certain Francis would have gotten so tired walking up and down those steep hills that he would have had to stop and rest (or quite possibly even collapsed unconscious from all the hiking). Chris imagines Francis to have been so dog-tired that he fell into a deep sleep, and that's when the animals would come near him. Only then could the creatures figure out whether or not Francis was asleep or had died from exhaustion.

After hiking for hours in this holy city, in the late afternoons we would rest our feet while dining on traditional pizzas and imbibing exquisite wines. My favorite meal was the pasta—pure perfection. You know it's prepared al dente when you feel it between your teeth as you bite into it. Assisi is magical in every way, the sacred *and* the profane. But it was certainly the lives of Francis and Clare that touched us the most during our visit. We just weren't prepared for how much *Clare* would make an impact on us.

Clare of Assisi was thirteen years younger than Francis. Born in Assisi to a wealthy noble family in 1194, she suffered from an absentee and abusive father. She died in Assisi at the age of fifty-nine. Before Francis's order was fully established, when she was just eighteen years old, she was the first woman determined to join Francis's marginalized band of poor brothers. In her time, this was unheard of. How could a woman join a religious order of men? Besides, Clare was from a prominent family, and she was expected to marry well. She had been groomed for marriage from the age of thirteen. Clare had many suitors but rejected them all. Societal propriety couldn't persuade her. She had a different call.

One day, cloaked in secrecy, Clare escaped from her parents' home to seek Francis's advice about familial pressure for her to marry her uncle's servant. Legend says that Francis encouraged her toward a radical life of poverty and prayer in service to God and humanity. Clare took his counsel to heart.

Later, on Palm Sunday, in the year 1212, undeterred by the attempts of others to dissuade her, Clare left her family for the final time. In the secrecy of night, Francis shaved Clare's head and embraced her as one of his community members. She was then put in two different monasteries for women before finally making her home at the Church of San Damiano, where she remained for forty-two years until her death in 1253.

Devoted to contemplation, Clare became known as a deep well to Francis's raging river. That well often sprang up as a "gift of tears." The gift of tears is a spontaneous and intense experience of God in which, when prompted only by the Holy Spirit, one is overcome with abundant tears. The episode leaves the individual with great comfort and often encourages those who witness it as well.

Clare was as committed as any of the brothers to a life of poverty and service, but being a woman in medieval times, she was restricted to cloistered life. She was not free to travel from town to town and country to country like Francis. Her vocation confined her to a simple dwelling where she devoted herself to prayer for Francis, the brothers, and the world they were serving. But it wasn't long before she emerged as a counselor to Francis and his brothers. Eventually, people from all walks of life sought her out as a spiritual director, including priests and bishops. Through contemplative prayer, she accessed a deep well of life-giving water to nourish the people. The calm depths of the contemplative life have an enormous impact on society at large.

Clare was a force to be reckoned with. She was the first woman to join the Franciscan movement, defying the dominant consciousness of her time that women were the "lesser sex." She embraced her equality with men. She was the first woman to write her own rules for her order. Men and women of all status turned to her for her wisdom and counsel. She embodied contemplation through extreme poverty, emptying herself to make room for the mystery of God in and through her. After Francis's death, Clare played a prominent role in preserving his charism and the Franciscan order. This was an extraordinary woman I was making pilgrimage to learn more about. As we journeyed to Assisi, little did I know about the encounter waiting for me.

The second day of our pilgrimage, Chris and I silently walked the three kilometers downhill to the Church of San Damiano to pray. Mass was taking place, and we slipped in the back of the small stone sanctuary and sat on the cold steps since the pews were full. The priest was speaking Italian, so I couldn't understand a word. But there was a presence in that place that gripped me, and soon I was overwhelmed. I couldn't hold back the tears. Something was happening to me that at the time I couldn't explain.

After the service, we made our way to the courtyard, and still I could not stop crying. Under the electric blue dusk sky, the silent, overwhelming tears just kept coming. The Franciscan priest who gave mass made his way over to me. He lovingly gazed into my eyes, put his hand on my shoulder, and spoke to me in Italian. The only word I could understand was *pace*. "Peace."

Soon the unearthing within me calmed enough to silently make the trek out of the valley, up the hill, and back into the village to our guesthouse. It seemed as if the tears poured out all night. Only later could I make sense of what I experienced. Some of that awareness came through the birth of my niece, Claire Jula (who coincidently shares the same name of Assisi's beloved saint).

I have nine godchildren, nine nieces, and one nephew. I uniquely adore each of them. Nonetheless, Claire will forever hold a very special place in my heart. Of course, all these children are cherished and special in their own right. Claire's distinctiveness expresses itself in her sassiness and natural musical talent. At just nine years of age she has the raspy singing voice of a seasoned jazz singer who spent a lifetime smoking. She's captivating. Claire has a way of making her presence known. She certainly did so the night of her birth.

It was a very cold and snowy January night when we got the call from Adam, Chris's brother. His wife, Winter, was going into labor with her second child. They asked if we wanted to join them at the hospital. Eager to offer support, we bundled up and met them in the maternity ward. There we sat with them while the nurse tried to make Winter comfortable. The minutes turned to hours, and soon it was the middle of the night. Winter was courageously and patiently progressing. Chris and I did our best to keep our eyes open, wishing there was more we could do to support Winter.

Then finally it was time. Chris was rushed out of the room as the nurses prepared for the baby's delivery. However, Winter said I could stay. Since I had no children of my own, I had privately hoped to one day witness birth. I was grateful for such a sacred opportunity. Winter was so brave and surprisingly calm. I was amazed. After a number of excruciating pushes, Claire Jula came into the world. Just like that. It was the most extraordinary thing I've ever seen. Winter, Adam, and I were elated.

Soon, however, we realized something was wrong. Claire was moaning. Not crying. Moaning. But the nurse said not to worry, "She's lamenting." It's an actual medical term. Claire was *lamenting*.

That day at the Church of the San Damiano I was also *lamenting*. It's not easy to be human and make our bold voyage through life.

Saint Clare gives us courage and teaches us how to draw from the depths of our potential to live our one wild and precious life.[4] If I had a patron saint, it would definitely be Clare of Assisi.

People have reported for years the dynamic energy of Assisi. In Francis and Clare, we have two incredible icons of male and female vitality. Few people are remembered eight hundred years later. But Francis's and Clare's lives made such an impact on this world that people still make pilgrimage to the place where they lived and died. In Christian history, after Jerusalem to visit the birth, ministry, death, and resurrection sites of Jesus, Assisi holds the greatest importance as a site of pilgrimage for the faithful. Usually, Francis is the one most acknowledged for emulating Jesus. But Clare is an equal luminary. It's her feminine quality that holds unique gifts for the world.

In Clare, we meet an icon of a deep well. Francis embodies a consecrated life in action, while Clare embodies a devoted life of contemplation. Certainly, both contemplation and action were integrated into the lives of each. But Francis is more a symbol for social action, while Clare illuminates the necessary component of contemplation.

Contemplative spirituality assumes depth. It rises from the deep well of presence, perception, and personhood. When nurtured, it overflows into streams of living water for others. Clare plumbed the depths. In her devotion to contemplation, she would have battled similar struggles as us to being present. But through rigorous spiritual discipline, she established presence of being. She stabilized the capacity to be in the here and now. From a young age she acquired clear perception, not settling for the expectations of family or society to be wed to a wealthy man. Clarity gave her the courage to pursue a radical vocation. Her name in fact means just that: "bright, clear."

Clare knew that her identity was not found in what she had, what she did, or what others thought about her. She perceived her identity as a child of God and lived into that identity with greater fullness as time went on. Freed from the shackles of personality, Clare established personhood. She lived into the reality of no separation from God or others.

> CONTEMPLATIVE SPIRITUALITY RISES FROM THE DEEP WELL OF PRESENCE, PERCEPTION, AND PERSONHOOD.

It is from these depths of presence, perception, and personhood that I and countless others have been able to encounter her living presence today. Her bodily form has passed away, but her essence is still very palpable—so tangible that she is still healing and freeing the hearts and minds of people all these centuries later.

A mere sixty years after her birth, Pope Alexander IV proclaimed Clare of Assisi a saint of the universal church and extravagantly declared her a saint of clarity and a clear mirror to the entire world. She mirrors to us who we really are.

Contemplative spirituality arises from the depths of reality. And no one demonstrates the power of a life rooted in this life-giving well better than Clare and Francis of Assisi. If Francis emulated a raging river, Clare embodied the deep well. In the two of them we behold an icon for contemplative activism. These luminaries radiate the way of Jesus. In them we see that it is possible to live Jesus' teachings and heal our world in our time. In particular, Clare gives us courage to plunge the depths of our souls and unplug the well, so that the river of life can freely flow through us to nourish our suffering world.

Practice: Labyrinth

Labyrinths were a feature found in some medieval cathedrals. They were once used as a substitute for making pilgrimage to Christian holy sites like Jerusalem, Rome, Santiago, and Assisi. One of the most renowned labyrinths is found in Chartres Cathedral in northern France.

The labyrinth is a contemplative prayer we practice by walking. It helps us traverse the depths of our inner well and find life-giving water. People who find it especially difficult to sit still for prayer often find the labyrinth to be particularly meaningful. There are also hand or finger labyrinths available.

Almetto Howey Alexander Labyrinth at the McCrory YMCA, Charlotte, North Carolina

The labyrinth is a unicursal path that facilitates the spiritual wisdom of losing your false self to find your true self. As you walk the path, it takes you inward toward the center of the labyrinth and back out away from the center. It mirrors the spiritual journey of descending into the depths of the soul and emerging to relate to the world with greater clarity and freedom. The path is walked slowly and contemplatively as a spiritual exercise of bringing mind, body, heart, and soul into harmony with God.

You can use the worldwide labyrinth locator at www.labyrinthlocator.com to find a labyrinth near you. Once you find a labyrinth to walk or a hand or finger labyrinth to use in the palm of your hand, proceed in this way.

1. Stand at the entrance of the labyrinth with reverence. You may prefer to place palms at your heart and gesture toward the center with a bow. You may also choose to remove your shoes as a way of acknowledging the sacredness of the prayer practice.

2. Ground yourself by taking a few deep breaths and state your intention or desire. For example, "God, draw me to yourself." "Free me from myself." "Give me perspective."

Your intention may be a prayer like this or may simply be a desire to be curious or playful, meditative or reflective. Invoke your intention.

3. Begin your walk. Determine whether you will walk fast or slow. A fast walk may help dissipate intense disruptive emotions. A slow walk may help create tranquility, leading to a meditative mind.

4. Continue to walk. Focus on intentionally placing one foot in front of the other. When you notice yourself distracted by thoughts, gently return to the intentional placement of foot to ground. Be present to the here and now practice of walking through the labyrinth. Let everything else go as you breathe and step.

5. Pause at the center. You may choose to sit or even prostrate yourself. Notice what it is like to have reached the center. You may choose to reflect or simply be.

6. Exit the center by walking back through the labyrinth until you arrive where you began. Express gratitude. You may like to recall the words of T. S. Eliot's poem "Little Gidding":

> We shall not cease from exploration
> and the end of all our exploring shall be to arrive
> where we started
> and know the place for the first time.

These steps can be easily adapted to hand or finger labyrinths. For more information visit gravitycenter.com /practice/labyrinth.

CHAPTER SIX

DYING FOR LIFE

The truth of the matter is, unless a grain of wheat falls on the ground and dies, it remains only a single grain; but if it dies, it yields a rich harvest.

JOHN 12:24

I have found the paradox, that if you love until it hurts, there can be no more hurt, only more love.

ST. TERESA OF CALCUTTA

NEARLY EVERYWHERE I TURN I see messages related to anti-aging. I'm more sensitive to these messages at this point in my life. I don't have the natural muscle tone that I took for granted in my twenties. My hips aren't as slender as they used to be. My hair is turning grey, my joints are stiff in the morning, and crow's feet are easily detected when I smile.

Recently, a friend from a national television news show came to visit. She was about to turn fifty, and she needed some time to soul search. She was longing for a career change, searching for something more meaningful to which she could give the second half of her life. During casual conversation, she mentioned how the news television industry is cruel to women over fifty. There are plenty of overweight, grey-haired men on the air, but older women on air do not turn profits for the network. She's not my only friend in the industry who has experienced such sexism and ageism.

Few of us have to deal with the pressures of public television. But the stress to stay young is experienced nonetheless. When driving down the main thoroughfare in Middle America's cities, billboards scream for my attention. They invite me to the latest remedy for reducing cellulite, hiding my grey hair, plumping up my lips, or decreasing wrinkles. Online advertisements are even worse. Anti-aging ads are a constant interruption that distract me from my purpose for being online in the first place.

I can't speak to the male experience, but I'm sure growing old isn't all that much easier for men. Receding hairlines, love handles, decreased sex drive, and the dreaded bifocals all remind them that their youth is fleeting.

Unfortunately, our society has made an idol out of youth. As if being young is somehow so wonderful. Sure, it has its gifts, just like every stage of life. But it also has its challenges. Our twenties are generally marked with trying to figure out where we belong, what group or community is best suited for us. We're relatively unsure of our self and subject to the expectations of others. We may be our most physically fit at this stage, with the glow of vitality, but we're usually far from being on top of our game spiritually and relationally. In our thirties, we may begin to experience some success at demonstrating who we think we are to the world. We find a way to establish ourselves in the group we're a part of. For others of us, though, we may actually begin to wake up and realize that we're not who we thought we were.

At whatever age we stop sleepwalking, once we've awakened to our illusions of self, a whole new chapter of life begins. It's much less about me and more about how to be of genuine service to others—without any kind of hidden agenda for power and control, affection and esteem, or security and survival. As the external beauty of youth begins to fade, we have the opportunity to discover within more of what the world needs: wisdom.

Wisdom generally comes with age, because it takes time and experience to learn the greatest lessons of life. The lessons that matter teach us what it means to be human: to love, suffer, lose, forgive, and love again. We learn these lessons through the grueling process of dying to our false self. It really does feel like death. When all you know is your false self, death of self seems like annihilation. Remember, to get something, you have to give something up. Growing old has its trade-offs if we're open to them. But we have to go further than aging to find the fruit; we have to die.

DEATH, A PORTAL TO THE DIVINE

One summer, I was invited by Father Richard to Saint Benedict's Monastery in Snowmass, Colorado, for the New Contemplatives Exchange. The previous year, at the invitation of Father Thomas, four of the most prominent living Western Christian contemplative teachers had gathered in that sacred valley. In addition to Father Thomas, OCSO, and Father Richard, OFM, Tilden Edwards, and Laurence Freeman, OSB, came together. Each of these men are recognized as being at the forefront of the Western Christian contemplative renewal, and each has founded a contemplative organization.[1]

These leaders were united in their shared commitment to the contemplative tradition and concern for the healing of our world. After their weeklong dialogue, they determined it was important to gather a group of younger contemplative leaders. A name for the gathering soon emerged: New Contemplative Leaders Exchange. It was important to the founders that this be a genuine "exchange," learning from one another and the Holy Spirit within each of us.

So, the following summer, I joined twenty other younger contemplatives at Snowmass, along with the four teachers who invited us. We were organized in groups of five or six according to the founder and organization we were representing.

It was incredibly nourishing to meet and dialogue with some of my contemporaries. After the meetings, some of us continued to grow in spiritual friendship. But what stands out to me the most from that week was my private visit with Father Thomas.

At the time, he was ninety-four. For several years, he had ventured to the brink of death and somehow returned. At the beginning of the week none of us knew how well he would be and whether or not we would even be able to see him. But surprisingly he was in rare form. His energy was up, and he was eager to meet all of us. Though his health wouldn't allow for him to participate in all of our meetings, he made a point to meet with each group that was representing one of the founders. Together with Father Richard, our group of six drove from the retreat center on the hill down to the monastery in the valley. As we approached, we turned on a lane with the ominous sign, "Cloistered. Do not enter." I felt like a schoolgirl breaking the rules. We were about to go into the private quarters of the monks.

After we veered around the bend, Father Richard parked the car, and we proceeded to file into the infirmary where Father Thomas was quietly living out the last of his days. As we walked in through the naturally lit corridor, we looked down the hall, and there he was. His towering, gaunt figure bent over his walker like a wizard with his staff. (He's always reminded me of Gandalf in *The Lord of the Rings*.) "Well, hello!" he greeted. "Won't you all come in and have a seat."

One by one, he embraced us as we all gathered around this aging spiritual giant. The windows overlooking the valley were behind us. Father Thomas was rightly positioned in front of us, with the opportunity to look out into the natural world as needed. I was reminded of the words spoken over me during my favorite mass of the year, Ash Wednesday: "From dust you've come and to dust you shall return." I wondered whether at Father Thomas's age the boundary line between flesh and dirt were less defined.

We were all spellbound. This man who had given his entire life away to prayer and service of the world had gathered us to be his guests for the week. Why? Why did he invite us? What was he hoping for in getting us together? "Well, I just want you all to know one another," he replied. He wanted to give us the gift of friendship with like-minded, like-hearted women and men who were concerned about advancing the contemplative tradition. What a treasure.

Father Thomas seemed to have so many questions for us. "How's it going?" "Are you getting along?" "Are you enjoying yourselves?" We had burning questions too. "How are you?" someone asked. "Well . . . I'm busy dying."

As our visit continued, we learned that it's difficult to die. Father Thomas was in pain most of the time. He revealed very little, but we could tell he was suffering—suffering but with a smile on his face. I sensed his suffering was intricately connected to partnering with the divine in a mysterious way (Colossians 1:24).

Another one of us asked, "What is it like to be busy dying?"

Father Thomas said, "Dying is becoming nothing. And that's not easy. It's the hardest work of my life."

By the end of our couple of hours together, each one of us was in tears, even Father Richard. We were speechless. It wasn't so much *what* he said but *how* he said it. His presence and his words penetrated our hearts. It was a transmission of essence to essence equal to that of meeting Mother Teresa many years prior. We were being changed, just by being in his presence.

As we slowly said our goodbyes and walked to the car, we were speechless. Weeping. That is what it's like to be in the presence of a person who has been deliberately learning to die nearly his entire adult life. Father Thomas had learned the art of letting go of his false self so that his true self—the self-united-in-God—could be free. It was like being in the presence of a seed that had fallen to the earth and cracked open. In the breaking open, the divine light was shining through him, for us and for the world.

Jesus said, "The truth of the matter is, unless a grain of wheat falls on the ground and dies, it remains only a single grain; but if it dies, it yields a rich harvest" (John 12:24). There's no way around it—following Jesus requires we learn to let go and die.

You who wish to be my followers must deny your very self, take up your cross—the instrument of your own death—every day, and follow in my steps. If you would save your life, you'll lose it, and if you would lose your life for my sake, you'll save it. What profit is there in gaining the whole world if you lose or forfeit yourselves in the process? (Luke 9:23-25)

Death to your false self is a necessary stage in the journey of transformation. And life will deliver exactly what you need to help you make this courageous passage of death and resurrection. Contemplative practice aids the process, for as my friend Drew Jackson says, contemplative spirituality is "practicing for death."[2]

The false self is the self that has a mind that doesn't understand, eyes that cannot see, and ears that cannot hear (Mark 8:17-18). The false self, Father Richard aptly says, is a poor substitute for our deepest truth. Jesus was referring to this false self when he said, "You must lose yourself to find yourself" (see Mark 8:35). We must lose or die to our *false* self so that we can find our *true* self. Paul used the language of old and new creation (2 Corinthians 5:17).

It's our true self that has a mind big enough for the contradictions and paradoxes of life: exercising faith when everything in us doubts, hoping when we're in despair, and loving when we're hurting. It's the true self that has ears that hear through delusion and eyes that see through illusion. But it takes time to awaken such a luminous identity.

Contemplative spirituality helps us acknowledge our need to die to our false self so that our true self can come to life—the self that is hidden with Christ in God (Colossians 3:3) and shines like the stars. We all sense and long for a more authentic identity, a truer *self*, beyond our profession, social role, or public persona. We inherently know that the self we manufacture is not big enough, that it is *small*, especially compared to the expansive life Christ desires for us.

The contemplative path teaches us how to die to our doubt, despair, and pain so that we can truly live in the realm of faith, hope, and love. In so doing, we not only find the meaning of life for ourselves, but we become vessels of vitality for others. Furthermore, if we can learn how to die now, we'll be well practiced and therefore more receptive to that final death. Then, our passing from this life too can be purposeful, and perhaps like Father Thomas, our dying will give others access to the divine.

Contemplative spirituality supports our Creator's mysterious work of awakening, healing, liberating, and transforming us. Through contemplative prayer, at ever deepening degrees, our defenses are dismantled and the burning flame of God's love breaks through our consciousness. That in-breaking is what Jesus called "the kingdom of God." In the kingdom we realize that we are safe, loved, and have no need to fear.

> THE CONTEMPLATIVE PATH TEACHES US HOW TO DIE TO OUR DOUBT, DESPAIR, AND PAIN SO THAT WE CAN TRULY LIVE IN THE REALM OF FAITH, HOPE, AND LOVE.

Over time, as we learn to let go into the divine through contemplative prayer, our entire being is illuminated. We begin to see with greater clarity a long and broad view; we grow in oneness with the divine and the whole created world; we love more freely and forgive more generously. Having freely received, we freely give. We become instruments through which Christ can heal, liberate, and transform the world.

BEFRIENDING DEATH

I'll never forget my very first visit to Kolkata, India (formerly Calcutta). The capital of India's West Bengal was founded under the British Raj in the 1700s as a trading post for the East India Company. Kolkata is the third most populated city in the world, and its streets and hovels are filled with a staggering 14.1 million people. You're surrounded by people everywhere.

Kolkata's noise and air pollution are among the highest in the world. Population density and mass poverty make this city the fourth most polluted in the world, following Delhi, Cairo, and Dhaka.[3] One study found that 70 percent of the population suffers from respiratory problems.[4] A 2011 report found that at least 70,000 people living in Kolkata are homeless.[5] Overpopulation and air and noise pollution, paired with a tropical climate, make Kolkata one of the harshest environments for a girl raised in Middle America to drop into.

Conditions were not that much different some sixty years ago when the modern saint Mother Teresa founded the order of the Missionaries of Charity. It was because of her that I made my first of many visits to this defiant city.

I knew very little about Mother Teresa growing up in a Protestant fundamentalist home. It wasn't until I met Chris that I simultaneously fell in love with her *and* him. Chris had met her the summer prior, and he couldn't stop talking about her. So, I read everything I could about the woman, all in preparation for visiting the city she made home and the work she carried out for those she called "the poorest of the poor."

Mother's words immediately captivated me.

With such simplicity, but with unmatched power, she drew me into her love for Jesus and her love for people in poverty. More than anyone I've ever met, she taught me how to see Jesus in suffering humanity. She was always reminding us to look for Jesus in the distressing disguise of the poor. By her witness, I learned that not only did Jesus identify with suffering people, he was incarnated in them. She was famous for reminding us with her five fingers of the five words that can change the world: "You did it to me" (Matthew 25:40).

After spending months growing acquainted with Mother through her writings, finally, like a dream coming true, I took the long journey from Indianapolis, Indiana, to Kolkata, India. I had heard many times how during Chris's first visit to Kolkata he worked at Mother's House for the Dying and ended up carrying out fifty dead bodies during his summer-long service. And I had read about this makeshift hospice house through the writings about Mother's work. It was the first home she established for people in poverty.

I had heard how there were fifty beds on one side for men and fifty beds on the other for women. These beds were reserved for impoverished people who would have otherwise died alone. The sisters would go out in the very early morning each day, combing the streets for people dying alone. They would find women and men in gutters and along train tracks, suffering an agonizing death. Then the sisters would bring them home, where they could die with dignity, in community, in the embrace of love.

I had heard all I could hear about this mysterious home where people are brought off the streets to die. I had to see it for myself. Like thousands of other people around the world, I was being called to visit there. Mother was incredibly hospitable to volunteers. She always said, "We need the poor more than the poor need us." I wanted to learn why.

So that summer, after adjusting as best I could to the scorching heat, the dense population, and the suffocating pollution, I got on a rickety, old, crowded bus and made my way to Nirmal Hriday, the Home of the Pure Heart or, as it is more commonly known, the Home for the Dying.

The road from the bus stop leading to the home was dirty and littered with trash. It was early morning, so some of the residents in the neighborhood were discreetly trying to bathe in the only possible place available to them—the street (a common occurrence in this overcrowded city). Others were beginning to open their small shops, undoubtedly praying for their daily bread.

The scenes and smells of the street were so oppressive that I couldn't wait to reach the home. Finally, there it was. Like a dim light in the midst of darkness, Nirmal Hriday welcomed me. Upon approaching the front door, suddenly I realized nothing I heard or read could have prepared me for this moment. At the threshold, through the closed door, I heard the most unbearable groans and moans. What in the world I had I gotten myself into? I wasn't sure I could enter. But the streets were not much more tolerable. So, trembling and praying for grace, I slowly entered to find breathing skeletons with skin on lying all around.

I've never been in the presence of so much death. It was terrifying. Coming from a society that fervently resists death, I didn't know the first thing about drawing near to it. I felt frozen. I couldn't move. Everything in me wanted to run, and yet something was drawing me in.

Soon, a volunteer took pity on my troubled state, came over, took me by the hand and showed me around. During the course of the day I learned how to feed the patients, how to scrub their metal dishes with ash by hand, how to hand-wash the laundry and change the bedding of the cots, how to bathe the women patients with dignity, and how to dress them with respect. By the end of the day, hot, tired, and full of meaning, I had been initiated into death and dying.

That was my first dramatic lesson in learning how to die. When I first approached the home, my programs for happiness triggered like fireworks. I desperately wanted some sense of power, control, and security. But instead of running to gratify those compulsions within me, I listened to the still, small voice that wanted something else. Freedom. Freedom to love.

I learned that summer how much we belong to one another and need one another. There, on the threshold of death, the patients needed me to help them eat and bathe and dress, and to remind them of their inherent dignity. And I needed them to help me find courage to resist the illusions that claim to provide happiness but leave me empty. I needed them to help me begin to unmask my essence. I needed them to help me find God.

NEW LIFE COMES FROM DYING

Those many years ago in Kolkata thrust me into the spiritual journey. Only later would I begin to grasp that *the way to live is to die.* It's not easy to learn this lesson.

There's something in our human nature that resists dying. To die is to let go of everything that attempts to define our identity and determine our happiness. We think we know who we are and what's good for us. But the truth is, we don't know who we are and what will ultimately make us happy.

Consumerism brings this to light. How many times have you purchased that piece of clothing or that book or that extravagant meal in the hopes of it bringing satisfaction? Once thoroughly consumed, you realize the ache you were trying to fill is still there.

Happiness is found in being free—free from our attachment to circumstances and possessions, and free from our compulsion to gratify our need for power, affection, and security. Liberation is found in the little deaths we surrender to every day.

When the doctor is concerned about your health and performs a test but you have to wait a few days to receive the result, this is an opportunity to die to your attachment to power and control. Everything in you wants to have power over the circumstances of your life, but suddenly this is out of your control. You have no power over the test results. There's nothing you can do to gratify it. You must wait. And in your waiting, you learn to let go, to die. In the dying you discover you are okay, no matter the outcome.

Or consider when you choose to speak your truth in some way—in conversation with someone or through a social media post perhaps. Your self-disclosure is met with disapproval by some and rejection by others. Suddenly your desire for approval is triggered, but there's nothing you can do about it. All of the acceptance in the world from others doesn't matter. It's only the negative responses that you remember. This is an opportunity to die to your attachment to affection and esteem. There's nothing you can do. You must wait and tolerate the distress of not gratifying your compulsion to be well liked. And in the enduring, you discover there's a part of you that is okay no matter what others think of you.

Or, God forbid, you find out one day that you're getting laid off from your job. What will you do now for work? How will you pay those outstanding bills? Everything in you wants to be safe and secure. But there's nothing you can do about it. The decision has been made, and you no longer have employment. As excruciatingly difficult as it is, this is an opportunity to die to your attachment to security and survival. You suffer the misery of not knowing where your next paycheck will come from. And in your suffering, you uncover a refuge that is safer than the circumstances of life.

Whenever our happiness programs are triggered, we have the opportunity to say yes to Jesus' invitation to lose our life as we know it. In the losing, in the dying, we learn how to trust in Ultimate Reality and root into the ground of being. We learn that nothing, absolutely nothing, can separate us from the love of God. We are in God forever and always. Life is hard. We will not escape pain. But the good news is that suffering and dying don't have the last word. There is a reality underneath the anguish that cannot be shaken. New life comes from dying, no matter how relatively small the death seems. A phoenix rises from the ashes, always.

> IN YOUR SUFFERING, YOU UNCOVER A REFUGE THAT IS SAFER THAN THE CIRCUMSTANCES OF LIFE.

Thankfully, in the process of moving from death to resurrection, contemplative spirituality supports us like nothing else can.

FREEING OUR MIND

The young men at the local prison teach me all about this. Regularly I venture to the Nebraska Correctional Youth Facility (NCYF) to lead a yoga class for incarcerated young men ages eighteen to twenty-one. This maximum-security prison is home for male youth who have been convicted of everything from theft to murder and sexual assault.

Men from all backgrounds take my class: African Americans, Latinos, Native Americans, and Caucasians. Occasionally, immigrants and refugees also participate. One of the saddest things I came to realize was the number of Sudanese refugee boys who have ended up in prison here. Having escaped the horrors of civil war with their family in hopes of a better life, it's terrible that now in the land of opportunity they end up behind bars.

Prisoners, like the youth in my yoga program, have likely endured more trauma in their life than we can imagine. "Trauma," Seane Corn says, "is anything that overwhelms our capacity to cope and leaves us feeling hopeless and helpless."[6] Studies indicate that many of the young men who attend my class have likely suffered traumatic instances in childhood, and some have endured prolonged or repeated distress. A large number of inmates suffer from post-traumatic stress disorder (PTSD). To make matters worse, prison rarely offers an escape from trauma as inmates fall victim to abuse within the facility. Living behind bars is at the least a very stressful reality.

Yoga offers an escape from stress and a way to be with the pain these young men have experienced. Few of the inmates probably grasp the full benefits of yoga practice. It's likely many come just to have some interaction with a woman. It makes little difference to me why they attend. Once they're on their mat, there's opportunity for them to heal.

The night before my first class, Chris and I had dinner with our friend Mariah. Mariah is a brilliant and spunky young woman. She has big dreams. She's determined to be a judge, and I have no doubt she'll accomplish that goal.

Mariah grew up in Omaha's inner city and attended an all-girls Catholic school. When she was just a junior in high school she'd rush from her last class to Gravity to make our weekly afternoon meditation sit. Can you imagine? How many of our lives would be impacted for the better had we started a contemplative prayer practice when we were a mere sixteen years old?

That evening over dinner, I told Mariah about the prison yoga program I would initiate the next day. Mariah listened intently and then looked me square in the eye and said, "Don't be doing any posture adjustments with those guys. One touch is too much, Phileena." "One touch is too much." Wise advice. I definitely keep appropriate physical boundaries. And the guys do too. Mutual respect is a hallmark of our class.

My teacher, James Fox, started one of the earliest prison yoga programs in the country. More than thirty years ago, with only a yoga mat slung on his back, he volunteered to teach yoga in the notorious San Quentin State Prison near San Francisco. Sadly, San Quentin boasts the largest number of death row prisoners in the country. It also has one of the most committed yoga programs.

I wanted the young men at NCYF to garner some inspiration from the yogis at San Quentin. So, during one of our classes I passed around some professional images of the San Quentin inmates in a yoga pose and asked my students to choose one that stands out to them and discuss it.

The youth studied the images. One of the photos was of a strong, brown-skinned man, with tattoos all over his body, balancing in the tree position, his palms together at the heart, eyes peacefully closed. In the foreground, you could see the bars of his cell.

Damien spoke up. "I like this one."

I responded, "Can you tell me why?"

"Because it reminds me that prison is in the mind."

We could have ended class right then and there. He got it. Prison is a state of mind—for all of us, whether incarcerated or not. Regardless of our circumstances we can either choose liberation or suffering within the confines of our mental attachments. Whether we're locked up or not, we all have to contend with our over-attachments to programs for happiness. Contemplative prayer frees us from these attachments, so that no matter what challenges life delivers us, we can respond to life with grace.

Opening to such grace requires we die to our self with its obstinate craving to be in control. As we lay down our self-will, we stop resisting what is and we stop clinging to what might be. It's in the acceptance of what is that we find freedom, contentment, and abundant life—irrespective of external situations, even prison.

AN ICON OF CONTEMPLATIVE ACTIVISM

No one knew this better than Mother Teresa. Born Agnes Gonxha Bojaxhiu in Albania in 1910, she left home when she was just eighteen to join the Sisters of Loreto in Ireland. After only one month in Dublin, she relocated to India to study and test her vocation to become a nun. By 1931, she took her first vows and changed her name to Teresa. Seven years later she found herself assigned to the Loreto community in Kolkata to be a teacher. But by 1946, at the age of thirty-six, she received another call: to serve the poorest of the poor. It would be two more excruciating years before she received permission from her superiors to do so. In 1948, the pope finally approved her request. She faithfully served this call until September 5, 1997, the day of her death. Her canonization to sainthood happened more speedily than most. Traditionally, it takes decades and usually centuries after one's death to be formally recognized as a saint. However, Saint Teresa of Calcutta was canonized in just nineteen years.

In her radical call to leave her homeland and later her religious community, Mother Teresa knew well the torments of the false self that clings to power, affection, and security. But her true self was well nourished by devotion and prayer and ultimately got the better of her. Saying yes to God was her anthem, no matter the cost. She definitely counted and endured the cost. She had to wait tirelessly on religious authorities to give her permission for that which she was being called. She was misunderstood by her sisters and superiors and later the international public. She often didn't know where the resources would come from to supply her needs and the needs of the children, women, and men in her care. Mother was well acquainted with the path of dying. In her dying, new life—life that rocked the world—came forward. By 1962, the nation of India honored her with the Jawaharlal Nehru Award for International Understanding. And in 1979, the entire world recognized her when she was awarded the Nobel Peace Prize. She received countless other recognitions from various nations and she even received the inaugural Pope John XXIII Peace Prize.

Like a grain of wheat falling to the earth, Mother Teresa died to her false self and ultimately produced so much fruit for the world that the entire human family had to stop and take notice. This is what a life can do when it learns how to die.

Death is the humblest gesture—yielding, surrendering to something greater than oneself. Humility is a sign of one who is committed to the spiritual journey. Commitment to the spiritual journey is a commitment to die to self. Even Mother Teresa's physical death was marked with such humility; Princess Diana died the same week, and so the news of Mother's passing was overshadowed.

Learning to embrace such a humble path took time. Mother's day-to-day life was a practice in dying. Like her sisters, she would pause five times a day for prayer. Unlike cloistered nuns with a strict vocation to the contemplative life, the Missionaries of Charity reflect more of a "mixed life" vocation. They are both contemplative *and* active. Wherever the Missionaries of Charity are established, they are connected to a home of some sort that serves the most vulnerable people in that area: hospice, children's homes, and the like. But without fail, in the midst of their very active service, they pause for mid-day prayer. I've never witnessed a more inspiring example of the mixed life vocation. The Missionaries of Charity embody it better than anyone.

It was Mother's unwavering commitment to contemplation (including Ignatius's prayer of examen) that made possible her radical life of surrender and fecundity.

Years after her death, right around the time Chris and I were starting the Gravity Center, I visited the Mother House where Teresa once lived. In the chapel at the house where pilgrims can pay their respects her body is laid to rest in a large tomb. At this particular hour, the room was nearly empty of visitors. I relished the solitude—just me and Mother. As I knelt at her tomb I was suddenly overcome with emotion. This woman who had touched millions and millions of lives also emphatically touched mine. I realized in that moment how everything I'd come to express around contemplative activism was directly related to her influence on me. I owed her my life.

My vocation is not nearly as radical or fecund as Mother Teresa's. But she, like all the teachers mentioned in this book, has been an important guide to help me find my way. Mother's witness to integrating contemplation and action helps us realize the invitation to die so that others might live. This is where the greatest meaning in life is found—in the freedom to let go of who we think we are. When we let go, we are brought into alignment with the divine

> THIS IS WHERE THE GREATEST MEANING IN LIFE IS FOUND— IN THE FREEDOM TO LET GO OF WHO WE THINK WE ARE.

will, so that in union with God we might make the world a better place. We cannot do that in our false, small, separate self. That kind of impact in the world requires our true, unified self. We don't get to that kind of transformation without dying.

A LIFE RESURRECTED

I had been to Kolkata several times as a young adult, pursuing Mother Teresa's spirituality and learning from her community. But without fail, every time I happened to be there, Mother was either ill and not receiving visitors or out of the country speaking to world leaders, a stark presence of sanity in a maddening world. The first few times I was denied meeting Mother, I was pretty disappointed. But in time, I thought such a gift was not meant for me. To diminish the blow, I convinced myself that I should not put her on a pedestal, that after all, she was only human.

I acquiesced my desire to meet Mother. Then to my surprise, one day while praying in the chapel at the house where she lived with her community, our beloved friend Sister Luke (an elderly Keralan nun from Singapore) hurried over and said they were bringing Mother out to receive guests. Now was my unexpected chance to meet the living saint.

Even though I had downplayed how special it would be to meet her, my heart leapt when I saw her being brought out in a wheelchair into the hall. Immediately, there was a dense presence, an energy that penetrated my heart. I couldn't hold back the tears. Trying to control the effects of her presence, I shuffled toward her with Chris.

There she was. A very broken and transformed human being that was pouring out divine energy. I was spellbound as she humbly took my hands in hers. I tried to impress her, telling her how Chris and I were following in her footsteps, caring for children with HIV and those orphaned by AIDS. But she wasn't impressed. She looked me in the eyes so tenderly and said, "Remember, your own children are the most important." First things first. Mother was always putting love in perspective.

She reminded us to not neglect those nearest to us. Of course, I didn't have the heart to tell her Chris and I were contemplating *not* having children of our own. We were discerning this difficult choice so that we could give of ourselves to the children in need who were already a part of our life. Instead, I just let her words sink into my bones. To this day, that transmission of her presence, of God's presence in her, has a way of prioritizing my commitments. I can't do it all. I can only do that which has been portioned to me. And that's enough.

Encountering Mother Teresa's charism, found in her communities around the world, was life altering for sure. But meeting her while she was still living surpassed all my expectations. To encounter Mother was to encounter Jesus. More than anyone I have ever met, Mother embodied the apostle Paul's words: "For to me, to live is Christ and to die is gain" (Philippians 1:21 NIV).

Teresa of Calcutta will undoubtedly go down in history as the greatest saint of our time—even though her biography reveals years of spiritual darkness and doubt. It is said that Mother may have experienced the longest recorded dark night of the soul—fifty years. Can you imagine? One whose life was undoubtedly fruitful experienced inexorable desolation and felt abandoned by God. She had heard Jesus' call, "Come be my light." And she became that light for the world, all the while living in felt darkness herself. In her private journals Mother wrote, "If I ever become a Saint—I will surely be one of 'darkness.' I will continually be absent from Heaven—to light the light of those in darkness on earth."[7]

One who lived in spiritual darkness was and still remains a shining light for countless others. While her life seems radical to most, Mother's spirituality is not only accessible to us but holds the keys that will unlock a life of impact. She illuminates so clearly that the path to life is found by dying.

Practice: The Welcoming Prayer

Dying in order to live begins with the wisdom to know what needs to die. The welcoming prayer helps us grow acquainted with how the false self is at work. It is a method of actively letting go of thoughts and feelings that support the false-self system.

The welcoming prayer was designed as an active prayer to accompany a commitment to the more passive centering prayer. In our daily life, our programs for happiness get triggered. We can usually detect we've been triggered because of the overly emotional reaction we experience to events. For example, we're going about our day and our inner waters are relatively calm, when all of a sudden something happens and our interior landscape is now turbulent. We experience difficult emotions like anger, sorrow, or fear.

In essence, our fight, flight, or freeze response is triggered. Our nervous system sounds the alarm that we are attached to some sense of not having the degree of power and control, affection and esteem, or security and survival that we desire. When this happens, we are not free to respond to life from our truest self. Instead we end up in reactive mode. Reactivity often stirs the turbulent inner waters all the more, leading at times to a downright tsunami inside that has the potential to spill out onto those around us, causing harm. The welcoming prayer helps us calm our interior waters so we can respond with grace to our circumstances.

Developed by Mary Mrozowski, one of the founders of Contemplative Outreach, the welcoming prayer invites God to dismantle the emotional programs of our false-self system and to heal the emotional wounds we've stored in our body.

The method of the welcoming prayer includes noticing the sensations, emotions, and thoughts in your body, welcoming them, and then letting them go. Practicing the welcoming prayer offers one the opportunity to make choices free of the false-self system—*responding* instead of *reacting* to the present moment.

The purpose of the welcoming prayer is to deepen one's relationship with God by consenting to God's healing presence and action in the ordinary activities of daily life.

When you have an overly emotional experience in daily life, take a moment to be still and silent and follow these steps.

1. *Focus.* Feel and sink into the feelings, emotions, thoughts, sensations, and commentaries in your body.
2. *Welcome* God in the sensations, emotions, and thoughts in your body by saying, "Welcome," to each of them.

3. *Let go* of each sensation, emotion, and thought, and
   finally repeat the following sentences:
   "I let go of the desire for security and survival."
   "I let go of the desire for power and control."
   "I let go of the desire for affection and esteem."
   "I let go of the desire to change this sensation
   /emotion/thought/situation."

For more information visit gravitycenter.com/practice
/welcoming-prayer.

CHAPTER SEVEN

UNKNOWING TO KNOW

Let this mind be in you,
which was also in Christ Jesus.

PHILIPPIANS 2:5 KJV

The universes which are amenable to the intellect
can never satisfy the instincts of the heart.

ANONYMOUS, *THE CLOUD OF UNKNOWING*

WE LIKE TO BE CERTAIN of things. We find security in knowledge. We like knowing that the sun will set tonight and rise again tomorrow morning. We like knowing that our partner or friend loves us. We like the independence our able body offers us. We like being certain about various aspects of life. But what happens if suddenly we are terribly injured, our friend betrays us, or, God forbid, the sun stops rising?

Years ago, Chris and I were enjoying a scrumptious dinner around our dining table with our beloved Jesuit priest friend Father Bert. Ignatius, founder of the Jesuits' Society of Jesus, understood that reform of the church depended on the reform of individuals. Consequently, the Jesuits played an important role in the Counter-Reformation.

Today, the Jesuits still abide by Ignatius's rigorous guidelines for spiritual formation. They stress that spirituality is not a privatized experience but a personal relationship with God that has direct impact on social change. Like Mother Teresa's Missionaries of Charity, the Jesuits are known for integrating contemplation with action. They incorporate a life of prayer with service, which often takes the form of education. Some of the best universities in the world are Jesuit.

Jesuits are sort of on the margins of the Catholic Church because they often get into trouble for pushing the boundaries of various doctrines and dogmas to get to the essence of transformational meaning for individuals and society. Father Bert was no exception. He often got called to the bishop's office to be reprimanded for not being strict enough with the laws of the church.

We just adored Father Bert. He was old and yet so young at heart. His mind was sharp, and he had a way about him that revealed he knew truth from life experience. It was the difference between the kind of knowledge that comes from intellectual study and the kind of knowing chiseled into a life well lived. That night over dinner, as we discussed politics, social justice, spirituality, and faith, he said something I'd never heard before. He looked at us with that twinkle in his eye and said, "You know, the opposite of faith isn't doubt, it's certainty."

What? I always thought the opposite of faith was indeed doubt, and therefore doubting anything about my religious upbringing or what my religion professed of God was nearly blasphemy.

But there I was, processing the cumulative pain of the world I had encountered during years of social justice work, and I was doubting everything. I doubted God's goodness. I doubted the teachings of the church. I doubted the virtuousness of American society and the justness of capitalism. It was as if all the paradigms I'd built my life on were crumbling beneath me. I felt like the man in Jesus' parable who built his house on sand. I had built my "house"—my identity, theology, and worldview—on sinking sand. And I was drowning in dust.

Thus began the unraveling of my life and my identity as I knew it. I had so many doubts that were coming to the surface, and I could no longer ignore them. That night around my dining table, I took courage in Father Bert's words; he hinted at the fact that I could somehow doubt and not lose faith.

Certainty, albeit something entirely different from faith, is an important part of growing up and constructing a life. In fact, there are three primary stages in the faith journey: construction, deconstruction, and reconstruction.[1] If we were brought up in a religious household, we were given the gift of a straight-forward, ideological system or container in which to begin to grow. The religious box offers us ideals and aspirations to live into and boundaries and limitations to steer us on a clear path forward. The security of some sense of certainty, then, gives us courage to set out on the voyage of life.

But when we have progressed and find ourselves on the high seas, the winds and waves of pain inevitably crash into our boat of certainty. The sky is dark, and the rain is harsh, and the tumultuous waves are overwhelming. At this point we might cling to our boat and deny our terror and pain. We may naively claim that God is good contrary to our experience, but that doesn't get us very far in the spiritual journey. Voyaging further necessitates bold honesty. And if we're truthful with ourselves, we'll raise the questions and doubts that rise to the surface. *Who is this God who torments with piercing rain, chilling winds, and drowning waves? I thought God was good! But if God is so good, why is God allowing this torment?*

It's at this point in the spiritual journey that we are invited to enter "the cloud of unknowing." Everything we were sure about gave us the courage to advance in the journey to this point. But now our certitude wavers. We've suffered, and we have doubts and questions. As we blink through the pounding rain toward the darkened sky, we hear a quiet invitation to enter what we don't know. This is the beginning of encountering Mystery.

It's one thing to know *about* God—our beliefs and doctrines; it's another to *know* God. When we enter the cloud of unknowing, we are forced to contend with suffering, doubts, questions, and the lack of answers for the complexities of life. Then, in time, we are drawn away from our over-dependence on intellectual assumptions and beliefs and into actual encounter with the Divine. Our certainties bring us to this juncture in the journey, but they cannot support the onward voyage. We have to find a different navigation system— faith instead of certainty. We have to learn how to be comfortable with what we don't know. Surprisingly, perhaps, it's by daring to let go of certainty and step into the unknown that our soul is most satiated. Think of the risks you've taken and the fulfillment that came from them.

Remember what it was like as a child when you first learned to ride a bicycle? Remember how terrifying and exhilarating it was when your caregiver let go of you, and the bike carried you forward? Entering the cloud of unknowing is kind of like that. It's frightening at first, but in time you realize you are held and carried

> IT'S ONE THING TO KNOW *ABOUT* GOD—OUR BELIEFS AND DOCTRINES; IT'S ANOTHER TO *KNOW* GOD.

by a presence much larger than you, and you realize you have capacities for cooperating with that presence. Over time you learn how to flow with that presence.

LIFE IS A GIFT AND LOVE IS THE POINT

Embarking on the turbulent seas of the spiritual journey began for me during my first visit to Freetown. Doubts and questions about God, myself, and the world around me flooded my boat. The scapegoating function of my early religious formation wasn't working well for me. There had to be a different way.

Soon after, I came across the renowned spiritual classic *The Cloud of Unknowing* and its included companion *The Book of Privy Counseling*. This small, unfamiliar book was written by an anonymous fourteenth-century English author, theologian, spiritual director, and mystic. It turns out this exceptional book of wisdom has captivated and guided its readers for more than 700 years.

This practical, timeless guide for Christian contemplation is written as personal instruction to a disciple who is well practiced and formed in Christian prayer and desires something more. The student wants something deeper, what the author directly names "contemplative." In the book, we learn early on that the contemplative path necessitates letting go of the faculties for reason, imagination, feelings, and will—the very senses we depend on to function with certainty. The author describes that on the path to enlightenment one must reject "all thoughts about *what* I am and *what* God is, in order to be conscious only *that* I am and *that* God is."[2] Central to the contemplative path yet so subtle is the process of letting go and learning to be with what is.

So there I was, in the midst of a crisis of faith, doubting the goodness and, quite honestly, the *reality* of God. And then it dawned on me. I had a profound impression that God wanted to reintroduce God's self to me. What I had known about God was taking a back seat to make room for that which I did *not* know from lived experience or direct encounter with God.

By this point, the doubts and questions that emerged in Freetown were just the tip of the iceberg of my unfolding spiritual journey. As time went on, I was faced with more life challenges and sufferings that plunged me further into the daunting seas of pilgrimage. I was learning to "walk by faith, not by sight." And boy, is that ever more difficult than it sounds. I wanted answers for my questions: *How could God let my friends suffer such exploitation, poverty, and injustice?*

> INSTEAD OF ANSWERS AND QUICK FIXES, GOD OFTEN INVITES US TO SIT IN THE UNRESOLVED PAIN OF IT ALL.

Have you ever questioned God like this? If you have, then you know that God rarely answers in the way we want. Instead of answers and quick fixes, God often invites us to sit in the unresolved pain of it all. On the spiritual journey, the answers to our greatest questions rarely come in a direct way. More often the answers come in unexpected ways, through many labyrinth-like twists and turns, descents and ascents—ultimately revealing a treasure hidden deep within. It usually turns out that our initial surface question served only as a probe to awaken us to an in-depth inquiry into ultimate reality.

Few of us are equipped with the spiritual formation needed for these times in life. I certainly had not been taught how to sit in the tension of what was, what is, and that for which I longed. And this is exactly what was needed if I would ever make it out of despair: a new way of being with life's pain and suffering.

In direct contrast to a widely accepted theory of atonement, I was led to let go of *redemptive violence* in exchange for *redemptive suffering.* This sheds great light on the meaning of Jesus' crucifixion and how it applies in our daily life. The cross reveals a way to hold the tension of pain, suffering, paradox, and evil. In this way, we learn how to overcome evil with good (Romans 12:21). When we hang in the tension between evil and good, we are stretched, and it feels like a psychological and spiritual crucifixion. But this alone is what will bring forth resurrected life—the kind of life that in the face of pain, suffering, and evil can genuinely extend hope, healing, and love.

Only the practice of centering prayer offered a cruciform way for me to hold these tensions. And so, I began sitting in silence for a minimum of twenty minutes two times a day. I sat and I sat and I sat as the days, weeks, and months pressed on. All that I had intellectually known about God (my belief system), my sense of self (my personality), and the world (my worldview) was absorbed into what the author of *The Cloud* calls "the cloud of forgetting."

As my mind with all its confusion and frustration slowly came to rest in the "cloud of forgetting," something beyond the mind began to rise up—what the author of *The Cloud* calls "naked love toward God in a cloud of unknowing." But if you are traversing this way, don't expect a "feeling" of love. What the author of *The Cloud* is trying to illuminate is not a feeling but a *mode of perception or attention.*

During crises of faith, all limitations of intellectual knowledge are exposed. We no longer have the answers. We need something more than rational resolutions. We need love.

Rational, intellectual knowledge comes and goes. As history unfolds, we learn more and we let go of things we thought we knew that are no longer true—like the presumption that the world is flat. The mind is limited in its ability and capacity to know, to have answers. Love, on the other hand, is infinite. It has no limit. Love is the energy and essence of all that is. Love conceives, births, creates, heals, forgives, reconciles, delights. Love is the midwife to becoming. As Father Richard says, "If God is indeed Infinite Love, then humans and all of creation are Infinite Becoming (which is the core meaning of 'divinization' or *theosis*, the process of salvation)."[3]

"Life is a gift and love is the point," my dear friend Ryan, a cancer survivor, reminds me.

Yes! This is what wanted to break through my turmoil all those years ago in Freetown—not answers to my doubts and questions, but love. In fact, the author of *The Cloud* calls the contemplative path "the contemplative work of *love*." But this "love" is less a feeling and more a *state of being* or *state of consciousness* from which we engage the world. Love in this sense is the ground or the center from which life flows. Love is the center of gravity that holds everything together.

In my distress, as I sat in solitude, silence, and stillness, I was slowly opening to love. It's as if the collective suffering I encountered in Freetown (and the personal pain I later encountered in my private life) stretched me in all directions. The tension created so much pressure that something new would be forced to break through. This is the reality of the cross. This is what living the cruciform life looks like. When we wake up to the reality of life with its pain and paradox, we hang in the tension of it all. We are pulled in every direction until a new heart (a new way of being) and new mind (a new mode of perception) break through.

The Christian contemplative way is about the mystery of the cross, the cruciform life. As Father Richard so eloquently puts it, this and only this teaches us "how to stand against hate without becoming hate, how to oppose evil without becoming evil ourselves." He goes on, "Can you feel yourself stretching in both directions—toward God's goodness and also toward recognition of your own complicity in evil? If you look at yourself at that moment, you will feel crucified. You hang in between, without resolution, your very life a paradox, held in hope by God (see Romans 8:23-25)."[4]

In my desperation, through the practice of centering prayer, I heeded the fourteenth-century spiritual director's words, and with fear and trembling pressed into the cloud of unknowing in the hope of redemption for our suffering world and my complicity in it.

INITIATED INTO LOVE

Perhaps, like me, you have experienced a crisis of faith or that necessary deconstruction phase in the process of growing up and taking responsibility for your life. That turn in the spiritual journey is when life really gets interesting. If we stay with the discomfort and disillusionment, we'll be initiated into the contemplative work of love.

Addressing this turning point in our pilgrimage, the wise and ancient spiritual director who wrote *The Cloud of Unknowing* describes the necessity of burying our faculties for reason, imagination, feelings, and will beneath a cloud of forgetting. Now this is a complete departure from the teaching of Ignatius, who, if you remember from chapter three, encourages us to fully engage the faculties in contemplative prayer. It's important to understand that there are different types of contemplative prayer, boiling down to primarily two distinct but complementary forms: *kataphatic* (prayer with words or images) and *apophatic* (prayer without words or images). Both forms serve the purpose of helping us progress on the spiritual journey through purgation, illumination, and ultimately to union.

The practices introduced in the previous chapters rely on kataphatic forms of prayer. In this chapter, we turn toward apophatic prayer.

Kataphatic and *apophatic* are sophisticated-sounding Greek words that give us understanding for the function of nonconceptual prayer (centering prayer, for example) that the author of *The Cloud of Unknowing* teaches. Kataphatic prayer comes from the Greek *kataphatikos*, which in essence means "with images or concepts." It is the type of prayer we are most familiar with in Western Christianity, also referred to as *discursive prayer*. This kind of prayer utilizes our faculties for reason, imagination, feelings, and will. We use words, images, and feelings to communicate with the divine. In this sense, God is mediated through our mental and affective capacities.

Apophatic prayer comes from the Greek *apophatikos*, which essentially means "without images or concepts." This kind of prayer lets go of reason, imagination, feelings, and will. And in this way, our encounter with God is unmediated. It is a *naked* mode of prayer—being to being or essence to essence without filtration through the thinking or affective mind. It's very strange for us at first because we have generally not been exposed to this way of prayer. Christian apophatic prayer is most similar to Eastern meditation.

Apophatic prayer is rooted in the doctrine of the divine indwelling (Luke 17:21; John 7:38; 14:3; Romans 8:10-11; 1 Corinthians 6:15-20; Galatians 2:20). While God is transcendent, God is also immanent, and chooses to dwell within us. Contemplative spirituality helps us realize God's presence within us.

The word *contemplative* derives from a root that means to set aside a place of worship or to reserve a cleared space in front of an altar. In Hebrew and Christian Scripture, a contemplative stance is obvious. The Israelites cleared space for worship with the Ark of the Covenant and finally with their temple. Jesus honored the temple worship of his Jewish tradition but also tried to enlighten his people to realize that sacred buildings, rituals, and rules are meant to bring us into the awareness of the divine presence in us and in all of those around us.

Jesus drew our attention to the doctrine of the divine indwelling in a radical declaration that he himself was the temple (John 2:19). The test of true worship, of true contemplation, according to Jesus, is seen in how we love God, our self, and our neighbor (Matthew 22:36-40), not in how good we are at showing up at temple or church for prayer and rituals. Paul elaborates on Jesus' teaching of the doctrine of divine indwelling by declaring that not just Jesus' but *our* body too is the temple of the Holy Spirit (1 Corinthians 6:19). How marvelous! The Creator of the universe resides within our being.

But unfortunately, we're not very well acquainted with God-within. We've mastered the theology of God's transcendence but have failed to embrace God's immanence. There's a part of us that doubts our deep connection to this divine love. Contemplative spirituality helps us overcome this disconnect. It's one thing to have a "personal relationship" with the transcendent Jesus—much like relationship with a friend or lover. It's quite another thing to become one with Jesus, by growing familiar with his immanence (John 17:21). It's from this oneness that enduring love of God and neighbor is possible.

I like the way Father Richard explains it. Kataphatic knowing comes through words and images, whereas apophatic knowing comes through the empty space around the words and images, allowing God to fill in the gaps in an "unspeakable" way.

Kataphatic prayer is the way of *knowing* and utilizes the dualistic mind, while apophatic prayer is the way of *unknowing* and exercises the non-dual mind. Both are essential forms of prayer for navigating the spiritual journey.

The author of *The Cloud of Unknowing* emphasizes that when we engage a nonconceptual or apophatic spiritual practice, we are admonished to put *all* mental discourse and reflection into the cloud of forgetting. This is the first and most critical step in the onward spiritual journey, because our mental-egoic mind (as Episcopal priest, scholar, and mystic Cynthia Bourgeault aptly calls it) is unable to navigate the path of love. The way of love often utilizes a different mind or different operating system (also a helpful metaphor from Bourgeault).

That other mind can be understood by extracting out of what we call "mind" two different forms of consciousness: dualistic and nondual. Dualistic consciousness is the predominant mind we utilize in everyday life. It divides the world into parts, into subject-object. It's rigid either-or, in-out thinking, concerned with exclusive resolutions. It's absolutely essential to living, and it is especially helpful in math, science, and determining whether to turn right or left. It's the mind that helps us make decisions and to function in virtually every activity of our day. The driver of this operating system is the self who is the subject, observing the various objects of her/his world and her/his experience.

Nondual consciousness from a Christian perspective has a different driver: the self-in-union with God. Contemplative spirituality supports the development of the nondual mind. The nondual mind enables us to live with the great challenges and paradoxes of life—those that generally center on the tensions at play in love and suffering, joy and pain. In contrast to dualistic either-or thinking, the nondual mind exercises both/and thinking.

The Christian understanding of ultimate liberation involves union of God and the self. As the self and God are "oned," boundaries and centers fade; all is one: God, self, neighbor, creation. No longer operating from the subject-object vantage point, life is now experienced from a whole different starting place—a place of union rather than division. When we access the nondual operating system, the unified, whole nature of reality comes into view.

The dualistic mind sees in parts, while the nondual mind sees in wholes. For example, when tragedy hits, the dualistic mind processes the pain by differentiating between the concrete circumstances of what was and what is lost. The nondual mind sees the bigger picture—through this loss, new life is born; *all* is not lost. We can at once grieve the particulars and maintain an open field of awareness for the larger possibilities at play.

It's crucial to recognize that the contemplative path nurtures the nondual mind, or what Bourgeault brilliantly calls the "heart mind." It's the nondual mind that helps us make the onward spiritual journey of overcoming paradox and contradiction. As we transcend ego, we are able to live into the highest ideals of our faith, such as loving our neighbor as our self, forgiving seventy times seven, and loving our enemies. In fact, it's arguable that much of Jesus' teaching cannot be lived without an established nondual mind or unitive consciousness. Simply put, the nondual mind helps us love.

When the author of *The Cloud of Unknowing* admonishes us to put all mental activity into the cloud of forgetting, his instruction helps us to let the dualistic mind rest and to activate the nondual mind. But at first, it's not easy to switch operating systems. It takes real effort, prompted by grace, to put the activity of the mental-egoic mind into the cloud of forgetting and let the nondual mind turn on. It doesn't come naturally for us. And so, we practice. Nonconceptual contemplative prayer supports us in this vital practice.

The author of *The Cloud of Unknowing* explains this fundamental contemplative practice:

> For although at certain times and in certain circumstances it is necessary and useful to dwell on the particular situations and activity of people and things, during this work [the contemplative work of love] it is almost useless. Thinking and remembering are forms of spiritual understanding in which the eye of the spirit is opened and closed upon things as the eye of a marksman is on [their] target. But I tell you that everything you dwell upon during this work becomes an obstacle to union with God. For if your mind is cluttered with these concerns there is no room for [God].
>
> Yes, and with all due reverence, I go so far as to say that it is equally useless to think you can nourish your contemplative

work by considering God's attributes, [God's] kindness or [God's] dignity; or by thinking about our Lady, the angels, or the saints, or about the joys of heaven, wonderful as these will be. I believe that this kind of activity is no longer of any use to you. Of course, it is laudable to reflect upon God's kindness and to love and praise [God] for it; yet is far better to let your mind rest in the awareness of [God] in [God's] naked existence and to love and praise [God] for what [God] is in [God's] self.[5]

Simultaneous to burying our faculties in a cloud of forgetting is a rising of our naked love toward God in a cloud of unknowing. Love that is naked is stripped of reason, imagination, feelings, and will. It is a cloud of "unknowing" because we don't yet know how to relate to God beyond our faculties. It is a "learned ignorance," as mystics like Teresa of Àvila and John of the Cross call it. And for a while we are transfixed between the cloud of forgetting beneath us and the cloud of unknowing above us. In between is mystical silence. This can be most difficult, for we feel as if God is distant or wonder whether God is present at all. The lack of employing our faculties to engage God leaves us feeling as if we are separated from God. But this only reveals that thoughts and feelings can be deceiving and highlights the limitations of our faculties prior to embarking on this path. Now is the time to let God introduce God's self to us as God is.

If pressing into the cloud of unknowing seems esoteric for you, consider something more down to earth. Any of us who are serious about following God or even just maturing as people have been faced with the opportunity to traverse the great "unknown." A job opportunity presents itself and you feel a tug to apply, but then anxiety sets in. There's so much unknown about whether you'll be called for an interview, and if you are, you don't know how the interview will go. If they offer you the job, then what? There's so much uncertainty about it all.

But by faith, or a hunch or still small voice, you take the plunge, enter the unknown, and apply.

Or consider the story of one of the women I meet with for spiritual direction. Argentine by birth, she ventured into the great unknown by saying yes to an invitation to work in Indonesia. At first, she was terrified. She didn't want to leave the security of her loved ones. But being very sensitive to the quiet voice of God, she took a big step of faith. Two years later, she experienced overwhelming gratitude because of the growth and wisdom that developed because she stepped into the great unknown. She reflected on the immensity of her trust in God— beyond what she can see, feel, or know. She is more rooted in trust. She now experiences trust as something she is grounded in, more than an objective feeling toward the divine. She also expressed what incredible peace fills her days now that she is rooted in the mysterious unknown that brought her to Indonesia. It's as if there are fewer limitations to who she is and what she can do for having followed that still small voice, letting go of her dependencies, and stepping into the unknown.

As for contemplative practice, the nature of an apophatic practice like centering prayer helps us let go of our dependency on our faculties and step into our own cloud of unknowing. These steps of faith free us of immeasurable obstacles that keep us from living into our fullness and potential for aligning with the purposes of God. We can grow, mature, and even deepen our trust in life, God, and the universe through life experience—like taking a risky new job or moving to the other side of the world. But contemplative practice stimulates and accelerates this growth and helps us make the most of the cherished time we have on earth.

Letting go of our faculties in nonconceptual contemplative prayer is so crucial because God cannot ultimately be apprehended by concepts, thoughts, and feelings. Our faculties, while useful for reflection and discourse, get in the way of direct encounter with God. It is naked encounter with the divine that leads to ultimate transformation, psychological freedom, and awareness of our union with God or unitive consciousness. Apophatic knowing simultaneously exposes the constraints of the dualistic mind and the expansive field of reality.

At a particularly challenging time in my life, I was faced with the invitation to either step into the great and frightening unknown or stay in what I knew and be miserable. I had a choice to make, and it felt as if I was damned if I stayed in my circumstances as they were and damned if I didn't stay. Sometimes, the greatest opportunities for growth and renewal can only come by way of stepping into the unknown.

It was terribly difficult for me to take that step. To do so meant I had to operate by an inner guidance system that doesn't rely on my rational mind or even my feelings. I could come up with all kinds of *reasons* to yield to the status quo or avoid stepping into the unknown. Yet there was a quiet and persistent inner nudge to find courage and take a step of faith in the dark. Unable to adequately see my way, I turned to my spiritual director, who graciously supported my process of discernment. Ultimately, she helped me stay in the present and determine the best next step. All the while, I couldn't put my hope in the future. The future was completely unknown to me. I could only *be here now* and literally put one foot in front of the other. Besides my spiritual director, there was only one friend in town to whom I could turn. Quinn was my saving grace.

Quinn and her husband, Paul Kulik, are the dearest of friends to Chris and me. Paul is a James Beard Award semi-finalist chef who has significantly elevated the food consciousness of Omaha, Nebraska. Quinn is a corporate attorney for Kiewitt, a Fortune 200 company. Their bright-eyed three-year-old son Hannes refers to our puppy Basil as "my brother." The two of them are bonded for life. On the rare Sunday evening when Chris and I are both in town you can find our chosen family drinking the finest of wine and the most delicious home-cooked food in the Kuliks' downtown row house.

Quinn is among a small circle of female leaders in a male-dominated multinational construction and engineering company. She's as tender as she is fierce. You really don't want to oppose Quinn during litigation. But if you happen to be within Quinn's personal circle of trust, she will care for you with relentless love. Lucky for me, I often find myself in Quinn's tenacious embrace. That winter was no different. As I stumbled my way through the dark, Quinn was there every step. She could see strength and courage in me that I couldn't see, and she would mirror it back to me when I doubted myself.

One day, in the darkest, coldest, most brutal time of winter, she surprised me with a twenty-five-year old jade tree. Standing four feet tall and four feet wide, it's stunning. I had always wanted a jade plant. I'd been drawn to them for years, but a hefty-sized one is quite expensive. The ones I'd seen had always managed to be just beyond my reach. Be that as it may, Quinn has a way of making dreams come true.

She told me the story of the lady who had cared for the jade at her plant shop, nurturing it to its robust stature and grandeur. Over the years, many people would drift in and out of the store. They would admire the plant and inquire about purchasing it, but the shopkeeper refused to sell it. She said no one was worthy of that tree.

Then Quinn told her about me and the difficult season of life I was in, and the woman's heart unfastened. It seemed Jade (as we call her) was meant for me. Quinn would let nothing stand in her way to bring that tree home to me.

Not only is the jade plant traditionally a token of friendship, it is also a symbol of growth and renewal. Today, the tree is a constant reminder that when I step into the great unknown, growth and renewal are upon me.

Like the serene and stunning jade in its arid soil, we too can thrive through the most desert-like seasons of life. To do so requires we tap into the Source that is beyond our felt senses and is closer to us than our breath. Guided by that alternative operating system (the "heart mind") into the unknown, we discover we are stronger, more resilient, and more capable of love than we ever imagined.

Encountering great love and connecting to it is how we experience the divine. Often, we don't experience God in a vertical, transcendent fashion. Instead, God comes in "sideways" as my friend Greg says. When we follow our Source into the unknown and our faculties struggle to know God's presence, this is the time to develop a different way of knowing.

Quinn didn't have to tell me "I love you" for me to know her love. The knowing came by way of encountering such extraordinary generosity and opening to it.

OPENING TO THE FLOW OF LOVE

I see the obstacles of the dualistic mind all the time when working with my spiritual direction clients. When a client is fixed in this operating system, they speak about a challenge in their life from their head, divorced from their heart and body—evidence that they are distanced from the lived experience. They're in subject-object mode. They are reflecting about it. If they stay in that manner of mental problem solving, they actually don't solve the problem. Rather, they get more stuck. Within the constraints of the dualistic mind, they are unable to break through with clarity and direction. It's only when the client begins to let go of mental discourse and get *inside* the experience (which usually means getting inside one's pain, but can also be about getting inside one's joy) that they encounter God and transformation breaks through. Let me try and paint a picture of this.

Recently I was meeting with a client in spiritual direction who was struggling to find joy in his vocation as a pastor and denominational leader. He was nearing the anniversary of his father's death and thought perhaps that was casting a shadow. In addition, he had recently turned down an impressive promotion with his denomination. As the session went on, we could have stayed on the surface of his life, at the mental faculty preoccupation, circling round and round trying to intellectually problem solve his lack of joy. But in that state, there is very little power and energy. The divine is kept at a distance.

So instead, we journeyed deeper into his story and what it was like when he first knew he was called to the priesthood. In the process of recalling these memories, he re-experienced a particular moment in his ordination service when the liturgist said he would find joy in serving and not in being served. Immediately tears welled up inside of him, and there was a tangible denseness to the energy of the room where we sat together.

There was now no longer any mental preoccupation between the client and God. The subject-object mental mechanism dissolved. In that moment, he was encountering the divine. He was in God, by being *in* his experience. As we continued on, he explained that serving for him has always been about being with his people. He compared himself to other clergy who aspire to grand accomplishments like publishing. Then he said that for him it's

> THE CONTEMPLATIVE PATH IS ABOUT ANALYZING LESS AND LOVING MORE.

all about love—about suffering with his people, extending compassion, being with them in love. Suddenly, everything became clear for him, and he realized he was lacking joy because he had not been with his people lately, preoccupied with other lesser demands on his time and attention.

God can only be experienced in the here and now. Divinity is the flow of love. Learning how to open to and be receptive to the flow of love is how change and liberation comes about in a person's life. So, the contemplative path is about analyzing less and loving more. The author of *The Cloud of Unknowing* makes it clear that God cannot be grasped by concepts, only by love. Contemplative practice helps open us to love.

As you can see from the story of this spiritual direction client, mental occupation and feeling have a place in the spiritual journey. But the mind and heart are most helpful when we develop the capacity to be present to what is, to let go of control, and thereby to become open to the presence of God that is always with us. It's not like God is somewhere far off and we have to somehow get to God. God is always with us, right here, right now. We just have to learn how to open to the grace that overcomes the obstacles that keep us from knowing God's presence. We do this not by our own willpower, but by responding to grace and cooperating with the divine. When we practice letting go of all thoughts, feelings, distractions, and preoccupations of the mind, we then learn to overcome the obstacles that keep us from God and our true self. Then we can move by faith into a state of unknowing, a state of open and receptive awareness, where direct encounter with God is more likely.

My puppy Basil teaches me this every day. He wears well his caramel brown coat with white fur down his broad chest. His chocolate-dipped snout is my favorite. And his captivating chestnut eyes gaze directly into your soul. He's strikingly regal. He was a rescue dog, but Chris and I feel he rescued us.

After seeing a picture of our little orphaned puppy portrayed as bashful and timid, we simultaneously saw deep courage in him and started to explore names that would reflect his daring strength. Of course, his foster mom had given him a name, but we wanted to rename him as a way to make him ours.

Basel was one of the first names we came across; it's an indirect Quranic name meaning brave, fearless, strong, courageous, and in some cases it's also used as "lion." Coincidently, the Greek name *Basil* (meaning royal, kingly, or "little king" in its derivative *basiliskos*) has been shared by numerous Roman Catholic and Orthodox religious figures throughout history that include church fathers, archbishops, priests, martyrs, and distinguished monks. In India, the herb *Holy Basil* is highly revered and sacred, associated with purification, protection, love, and eternal life. It holds special importance for me because it has been an essential antidote for healing my body's endometriosis. In the short time Basil has been a part of our family, he's helped us heal and find courage, especially in the face of the unknown.

Basil naturally reminds me to be here now and helps me find God in the present moment. When we first adopted Basil, I knew I needed to be in nature more. So I was thrilled to realize he would thrive best if walked three times a day. His needs force me to nurture my own. So together we get into the great outdoors and commune with God in the created world.

During one of our morning walks, Basil invited me to pause and pay attention to the wind in the trees. And you know what we heard? "Welcome home. All living things are your family. You are safe. We belong together. All is one." And then Basil heard something quite mysterious, and we were suddenly caught up in the sacredness of the universe. Before we got too transcendent, Basil spoke to me as only he can do with that determined, purposeful bark, and we found our feet on the ground, in the tall green grass, the cool breeze caressing our faces, grateful to have each other and this world we call home. Life is just better with Basil. He brings me so much joy.

I can relate to my spiritual direction client's desire for joy. After making such an impactful transition from what Chris and I refer to as "our former life," I struggled for a few years to find joy. I knew I had made the right decision to leave our previous organization and start Gravity, but I was grieving a lot of losses. And in that season of grief, I lacked joy. So, I began praying that God would give me joy, and God surprised me by giving me Basil. My life will never be the same. Basil helps me to discover God anew and to open at ever-deepening levels to love.

The contemplative path is a work of love. It is exercising our relentless love of God through the path of unknowing, and opening to God's unconditional, all-consuming love of us. All the while, contemplation anchors us in love as a state of awareness (knowing) or mode of perception from which our active life takes shape and expression. Being rooted in love requires we progress through unknowing to be stabilized in a knowledge that is not limited to the intellectual mind, but instead permeates the very fibers of our being.

Practice: Centering Prayer

Centering prayer roots us in divine love. It is a modernized prayer method based on the intuitive prayer rooted in lectio divina and *The Cloud of Unknowing*. It is a method of silent prayer that prepares us to receive the gift of contemplative prayer—prayer in which we experience the divine's immanent presence with us. Centering prayer is grounded in relationship with God, through Christ, and is a practice to nurture that relationship.

Unlike other prayer practices, in centering prayer we are not looking for an insight, impression, takeaway, or any other experience. This is a nonconceptual prayer practice and therefore very different from most other forms of prayer we've experienced. It is a Christian form of meditation, a practice in letting go of thoughts, feelings, and sensations.

Centering prayer complements and supports other modes of prayer—verbal, mental, or affective prayer. It facilitates resting in the divine presence. Centering prayer offers a way to grow in intimacy with God, moving beyond conversation to communion.

As Father Thomas emphasizes, the source of centering prayer, as in all methods leading to contemplative prayer, is the indwelling Trinity: Father, Son, and Holy Spirit. The focus of centering prayer is the deepening of our relationship with the living Christ. The effects of centering prayer are ecclesial, as the prayer tends to build communities of faith and bond the members together in mutual friendship and love. To practice centering prayer, follow these steps.

1. Sit in an upright, attentive posture in a way that allows for a straight spine and open heart. Place your hands in your lap.

2. Gently close your eyes and bring to mind your sacred word, image, or breath as your symbol to consent to

the presence and action of God within you. Your sacred symbol is intended to be the same every time you pray. It helps to ground you in the present moment. It allows you to give your undivided, loving, yielded attention to God. Choose a name for God or an attribute of God like love, peace, and so on. You may prefer a sacred image instead or simply a mindful breath.

3. Silently, with eyes closed, recall your sacred symbol to begin your prayer. As you notice your thoughts, gently return to your sacred symbol. Do this however many times you notice thoughts, feelings, or sensations.

4. When your prayer period is over, transition slowly from your practice to your active life.

It is recommended to pray in this fashion for a minimum of twenty minutes, two times a day. Start out slowly with initial prayer periods of five to ten minutes, then work up to the desired length of time.

During a visit with Father Thomas, he commented that two thirty-minute sits is a good *start*, implying that if we can manage to come up with more time each day, then all the better. Do what works for you. Start with a time limit that is manageable and attainable, and grow your practice from there by the leading of the Holy Spirit.

For more information visit gravitycenter.com/practice /centering-prayer.

CHAPTER EIGHT

WAKING UP

Therefore, stay awake, for you do not know
on what day your Lord is coming.

MATTHEW 24:42 ESV

Faith does not need to push the river
because faith is able to trust that there is a
river. The river is flowing. We are in it.

RICHARD ROHR

EACH YEAR, GRAVITY hosts a Deepening Retreat at the Benedictine monastery just outside Omaha, Nebraska. People travel from all over the country and from around the world to gather with us for this annual retreat weekend. Some make it a point to attend every year, as a way of resetting their commitment to the contemplative path. The Deepening Retreat is for people who want to grow more acquainted with silence. Besides the opening and closing sessions, we spend about forty hours in mostly what we call "grand silence." Though we meet together for meditation sits, brief teaching, and yoga practice, we do not speak to one another. Instead, we cultivate reverence and support for one another's soul-searching and prayer.

One spring, I noticed that my friend Adrian had registered. Adrian is one of the most intriguing men I know. A Harvard graduate, Adrian led the international growth of Comedy Central and *Saturday Night*

Live (*SNL*) in broadcast markets around the world. He's a dynamic extrovert—outgoing, whimsical, and full of energy. He's one of those men who just captures your attention. He's incredibly brilliant and can talk to anyone about most anything. It's impressive to see him work a room with magnetism and charm.

Adrian is many things, but *quiet* is not a description I'd readily give him. He avoids silence. So, when he signed up for the Deepening Retreat, I wondered how he'd manage. He wondered too. I saw him a few times before the retreat weekend, and he peppered me with questions, trying to figure out if he could handle so many hours of silence. He thought, if *he* could do it, *anyone* could.

During the opening session, I could tell he was nervous about what was coming—forty hours of no talking, forced to be alone with the thoughts in his head. Everyone shared their intentions for the retreat, and though I don't remember his precise words, I do remember how very important the weekend was for him. I remember he shared how terribly difficult it would be for him to not talk but that he knew he needed this retreat and was willing to rise to the challenge.

These Deepening Retreat weekends are pretty difficult for most people at first. Our society is full of so much noise, it's rare for most people to get even five minutes of silence, let alone forty hours. And while modern technology seems to crowd out the quiet, most of us consciously or unconsciously *avoid* it. We do whatever we can to keep busy, noisy, and . . . well, distracted. Distracted from what's going on inside of us; distracted often from truth. Because before truth is freeing, it's usually painful. We resist pain. We'd rather not go there. So, we keep busy, noisy, and distracted.

During a Deepening Retreat weekend, you can avoid your inner life for only so long before you're forced to face it. And thankfully, you're being held by a group of people who are on the same journey for truth and freedom as you. You're not alone. And that makes facing your truth a little easier.

During the closing session, as usual, we invited everyone to share a gift and challenge from the weekend. Sometimes it takes a while for someone to break the silence and begin sharing. But not this time. Adrian could not wait to start verbally processing what it was like to make this formative retreat. Within moments he shared one of the most profound insights about silence that I've ever heard.

When he worked at *SNL*, Adrian got familiar with the qualities of a recording studio and the necessity of paying attention to *room tone*. Room tone is also known as *presence*. It's the sound in a room that is recorded when no dialogue is spoken. When there is silence, we can detect room tone or presence. It's proven and recordable. There really is another dimension of energy going on underneath the noise with which we're most familiar. Adrian explained it this way:

> Every recording studio in the world (in fact every room in the world) has its own room tone or presence. It's the sound of a room when all the instruments and amplifiers are turned off. There's a very low throb that is always in the background. And you can't hear it when other noises are going on. You have to turn everything off, and then you can sense it. God is the drone note that underscores everything. And you have to turn off a lot of distractions if you want to hear it.[1]

"God is the drone note that underscores everything." But we have to get quiet to notice that presence.

In solitude, we learn to be present.

In silence, we learn to listen.

And in stillness we develop restraint.

Contemplative prayer, held by the postures of solitude, silence, and stillness, helps us wake up to Presence. Regular contemplative practice helps us detect the "room tone" or the "drone note" undergirding our life. Once that presence is recognized we can more easily discern how to respond to life. Even just a little contemplation goes a long way. The important thing is to awake from our slumber and stop resisting this critical part of life. It's time that all of us who desire to build a better world make time for spiritual practice. The future of our global family is counting on it.

Clearly, we all need at least a little bit of solitude, silence, and stillness. And some of us will be called to more. I think the human family has a way of compensating for one another. We all have work to do to heal our world. While some will lean more heavily into action, others will take up more contemplation. For those of us who are called to more contemplation, we may at times desire extended amounts of solitude, silence, and stillness, perhaps even seasons of hermitage.

> IT'S TIME THAT ALL OF US WHO DESIRE TO BUILD A BETTER WORLD MAKE TIME FOR SPIRITUAL PRACTICE.

HERMITAGE IN THE BLOOD OF CHRIST MOUNTAINS

I first heard of the concept of hermitage many years ago when I visited the Abbey of Gethsemani where Thomas Merton lived. Hearing of his experiences in extended solitude and silence mesmerized me. I craved it. As time went on, I learned of others who dared to go deep into sacred solitude and silence through hermitage—people like Francis of Assisi, whose primitive hermit cave can still be visited today. Tucked away in the forested hills surrounding Assisi, Italy, you'll find it. The cave is so small you have to bend over in humility to enter it. Solitude, silence, and stillness are quite palpable in that place. It was here that Francis was known to have prayed often throughout the night, "Who are you God and who am I?"

For most of my adult life, I've been called to take regular time away from family, friends, and the normal routine to devote myself to soul searching and soul healing through prayer. Usually that means withdrawing from my normal surroundings by retreating to a monastery of some sort. Occasionally, it has meant more dramatic isolation from all people, more like hermitage.

And so, one year, I determined to make hermitage at the Lama Foundation near Taos, New Mexico. It was quite a journey to get there. I had to fly from Omaha, Nebraska, to Albuquerque, New Mexico, and spend the night. The next morning, I rose early at 5:00 a.m. so I could prepare to make the three- to four-hour trek to the Sangre de Cristo (Blood of Christ) Mountains. I couldn't imagine a more fitting destination for retreat.

Lama recommended Twin Hearts shuttle to drive me from Albuquerque through Taos to the mountains. So, when the time arrived, a middle-aged native man came to the lobby of my hotel and carried my suitcase to the big, white, unmarked, beat-up, twelve-passenger Dodge van. The vehicle was full of young Spanish-speaking people and a retired white man from Texas who used to work for NASA. To my delight, the only seat available was the front passenger one. Perfect. I could have a good view of the drive, albeit for the big crack in the windshield.

The driver, Robert, was also the owner of the shuttle business. Twenty-five years ago, when he was trying to think of a name for his business, he looked up and saw the Sacred Heart of Jesus and the Immaculate Heart of the Blessed Mother. Ta-da. Twin Hearts. Not long after that, a woman received a vision from Jesus saying that nothing would destroy his business, though he would go through many trials that would threaten his livelihood. He said the good Lord promised him that his business would succeed. And sure enough, it's still going. Good thing, because his is the only shuttle company that will go to the hard-to-reach destination of Lama.

We were on our way. We would eventually make stops in Santa Fe, Taos, and Lama, and then the van would go on to a town called Angel Fire. I knew it was going to be a long day, so I settled in and got comfortable with my humble surroundings. I anticipated the journey ahead with some apprehension. The weather was predicting a snowstorm with up to twelve inches in the mountains, right where I was headed.

As the day unfolded, we navigated through the breathtaking Rio Grande gorge and climbed higher and higher into the snow-kissed peaks. When we approached Lama, Robert pointed to the far-off buildings in the crest of the mountains and, with pride, said, "There it is. That's where you're going."

We were running about an hour behind schedule, and by the time we reached Lama it was nearing sunset. The road into the one hundred acres that make up the Lama commune was narrow, unpaved, thick clay ("lama"). Robert informed me that if it snowed as predicted, someone would have to drive me down to the main road on the return because the van wouldn't be able to make the drive up.

When we reached the top, Bird was there to welcome me. Yes. That's really her name.

Bird looked to be in her early sixties, well endowed, with grey, unkempt hair, wearing dirty jeans, a well-worn grey sweatshirt, and a blue stocking cap that sat loosely on top of her head. She had lived at Lama in the nineties for about five years and from time to time returned as she "felt called," she said.

With generous hospitality, she welcomed me into the kitchen, served me fennel tea and biscotti, and hurried to get me settled before the sun went down. After I finished tea we went to the larder (cellar), where I chose potatoes, beets, carrots, onion, chard, squash, avocado, orange, apples, and pears for my sustenance during my stay. Dried goods were waiting for me at the hermitage.

With food in one hand and luggage in the other, Bird led me out of the kitchen and through the forest along a narrow path to "Bear Hermitage." She pointed out deer tracks along the way. She also showed me the tall, covered silver can where I could leave my request for provisions each day by noon and collect them by 3:00 p.m. the same day. In this way, I would not be disturbed and not see any other people during my stay. As we neared the hermitage, she directed my attention to the compost outhouse. She explained that I would flush it with the straw in the bin next to the hole where I'd deposit my waste.

After an exhilarating walk carrying my luggage, we made it. Just in time for sundown.

Bird built me a fire in the wood stove, made sure the kerosene stove-top was working, directed me to the dry goods and tea provided, pointed out the cans of water for drinking and washing, made note of the pee-bucket, and then scurried off. She was deliberately trying to respect my time in sacred solitude, silence, and stillness. As she hurried away, she promised to check on me the next day to be sure I didn't get snowed in.

Exhausted from the long day of travel, I melted into the hermitage. It felt effortless to sink down into the present moment. I lit the oil lamp and did my best to prepare a hot meal of lentil-carrot stew with brown rice.

I'm no camper. But I imagine this would be a camper's dream. There I was, out in the middle of the mountains all alone. I had left modern society far, far behind. A cozy, warm shelter was provided, stocked with wood for burning, kerosene for cooking, and provisions to boot.

I soon came to learn, with the help of a journal provided for visitors, that the carefully crafted hermitage was a vaulted straw bale house, built by hand in silence, by eight women from as nearby as Taos and as far away as Tokyo. During construction, every hour a bell was rung and the builders sat still in mindfulness for five minutes. This helped the builders return to the present moment. The work was done as spiritual practice, and it stands as a witness to the integration of prayer and service, spirituality and work.

When the foundation was ready, the woman from Tokyo taught the others how to draw Japanese characters on rice paper for intentions such as joy, harmony, love, and abundance, and each blessing was put into the foundation for all the future hermits. I never felt more support during a private retreat.

The vaulted straw bale hermitage, built with limited lumber and only the energy expended by human activity, leaves a very tiny eco footprint. Since it's extremely well insulated, it's incredibly energy efficient. It requires very little from the earth to sustain it.

As it turns out, the hermitage was named for a cinnamon-brown, female adolescent bear that was killed on the Lama property at the time of construction. Sadly, the last grizzly bear in the area was killed around 1950, but there are still many black bears. The story is that one of the Lama guests chased the young female bear up a tree. The game warden was called, and eventually the bear was shot—once in the jaw and then a second time, which brought it tumbling thirty feet down to the ground to her death.

The builders report that the next day the land felt stiller, drier. They built while mourning the needless death of the innocent creature. In the distance a white mockingbird cried the entire day.

The builders wished to make the point that modern society is fabricated on an economy that overlooks nature, health, well-being, and enlightenment; that we are not only out of sync with the natural world, but we are *destroying* it. Their mission and witness, like Lama's, is to dream of a better world where we live in harmony with nature, doing no harm, taking only what is needed, and giving back in symbiosis.

In Bear Hermitage, I found myself embraced in a vision that cries for a more peaceful, harmonious world.

Interestingly, the room tone felt like a warm womb.

Taking in my surroundings and everything I had already received, I laid down heavy on the elevated bed, listened to the roar of the wood-burning stove, snuggled under the down comforter and heavy quilt, and gazed out the huge bedside window at the spectacular starlit sky. I felt held, connected, and hopeful. It was 8:00 p.m. The following poem emerged from somewhere deep down inside my soul:

> Here in your womb I am safe
> I let go and find I am held, connected
> You nourish me
> I find rest

I become a child again
Naked, unafraid, free
You soothe me
And I re-member
The fragmented, separated parts of me
You knit back together
And I remember nothing can separate me from you
A secret, hidden work
Here in your womb.

When I awoke the next morning at 4:30, the clear sky had turned dense white, and I found my hermitage blanketed beneath fresh, thick, soft snow. I couldn't help but think of Bear for whom the hermitage is named. This creature that God gave us, what might she have to teach me?

Native spirituality holds on to what—but for the few luminaries like Francis of Assisi and Tielhard de Chardin—Christian tradition has predominantly neglected: a deep appreciation for the created world and the interconnection of all beings.

Bear, like all animals for Native people, has a special meaning. Bear is symbolic of grounding, strength, and confidence—all qualities that I was very much needing at the time. She inspires courage against adversity. She takes action, and she leads. Bear promotes physical and emotional healing and reminds us to take time for solitude, quiet, and rest. Here I was, in this hermitage, being drawn to consider Bear as a teacher. And these thoughts stirred in me:

Bear is dominant yet gentle.
She fills the space she inhabits but treads softly.
She lives her life contentedly with fierce love.

Bear's meaning speaks very personally to me. As I've attempted to yield my life in ever-deepening ways to God, I've been called to stand my ground in the face of adversity. I've been inspired to lead and take action in spite of historical, religious, and cultural paradigms that disapprove of my truth and the expression it takes in my life and faith. The call has demanded incredible courage. As my friend Breanna once noted, "Courage is speaking your mind with all your heart." Courage isn't the absence of fear but facing your fear head on and not backing down—like a mama bear.

During hermitage, a greater desire for *fearlessness* rose in me. I've faced my fears time and again. That has served its purpose—growing me up in quiet confidence and strength. I am resolved to be free of fear, to be unafraid. To boldly and humbly live this one wild and precious life I've been given. To do so requires I stay awake and stay true to the most authentic parts of the divine presence and expression in me.

MY AWAKENING, YOUR AWAKENING, OUR AWAKENING

During hermitage, as the days unfolded I found myself drawn to deep rest, retiring by 8:00 p.m. and waking at 5:00 or 6:00 a.m. After building the early fire, I'd commence my morning prayer with a fifty-minute sit, followed by lectio divina, spending three to four hours in centering prayer throughout the day. The sun would make it over the crest of the mountain about 8:30 a.m. Then I'd find myself stretched out on the bed soaking in the warmth of Sun's rays, in perfect presence, peace, and gratitude to be alive, breathing, feeling . . . being.

In between prayer sits and preparing meals I finished a few good books. Eventually, I ventured out for a couple dreamy, snowy walks.

At Lama, I found the grace of being present to be so profound that I had very few reflective moments. The following words I'd come across in past readings reverberated in me.

> God is my center when I hem Him in
> My circumference when I melt in Him

It's only now, after emerging from hermitage, that I can reflect on the experience, mining for the gold that was deposited during such sacred time. And yet, there were a few moments of in-breaking where desire, prayer, and poetry from the depths of my being uttered forth. Here's one such moment:

> Let it be done to me according to your Word
> Let me be a womb for you
> Come Lord
> Be conceived in me anew
> Fill me up with Your presence
> And then break me open in your process of redeeming* the world.
> (*at-one-ment/return to unity)

Truly, this kind of at-one-ment is God's desire and God's work. We are in the process of being redeemed, being brought back into unitive consciousness. That conversion begins by waking up from our illusions that keep us fragmented and separated from oneness. We must realize our fundamental identity as being part of a whole—interconnected— not separated or cut off from God or one another. This was Jesus' explicit prayer for us (John 17:21). Awareness of oneness is what it means to be a part of the Body of Christ. We are one body. We live and move and have our being in a unified field of love. When more of us awaken to this reality, the world will be a better place.

Life is short. Our human family is destroying itself and the planet. Our destruction of one another and the world we live in is a result of sleep walking in our sense of separateness. We are unconscious. "Abba forgive them. They don't know what they are doing" (Luke 23:34).

It's time to wake up and nurture unitive consciousness through contemplative practice. Through contemplation we realize our potential for reflecting our divine heritage. Meditation practice helps us access greater capacity within for love, joy, peace, patience, gentleness, goodness, faith, meekness, and self-control (Galatians 5:22-23)—all virtues readily available to us when we are awake and aligned with the divine. Now is the time to wake up. Now is the time for more healers, liberators, and peacemakers (see Matthew 5:1-11).

The awakening and renewal of the human family, the very body of Christ, begins with each of us. To the degree *I* am healed, free, and at peace, the *world* is healed, free, and at peace.

Christ's suffering, death, and resurrection was a historical, particular act, yes, but a cosmic one too. The work was finished and is being finished. Perhaps now more than any other time in human history, we are caught up in a divine dance of remembering who we are. Our personal and collective consciousness is evolving; we are slowly taking on the mind of Christ (Romans 12:2; 1 Corinthians 2:16; Philippians 2:5) and growing toward personal and collective wholeness. We are being made new (Galatians 2:20; 2 Corinthians 5:17; 2 Peter 1:4). But even as we are being made new, the world around us seems to be destroying itself.

After nearly two thousand years of Christianity, nations are plagued with brutal exploitation, horrific war, and the destruction of our planet. Our human family is fragmented by fear, suspicion, and judgment of one another. We are far from living like the unified sons and daughters of God that we are.

Think about it. As children of God, we have divine DNA. We are created for magnificent purpose in the world. Human evolution has helped us embrace the wonder and gifts of the rational, intellectual mind. Humanity has achieved remarkable heights in scientific exploration and scope. The intellectual mind offers solutions for some of the world's greatest problems. Yet, we are still falling short—a far cry from doing even greater things than Jesus, like he said we would do (John 14:12). Utilizing only the intellectual mind will not do. We also need to employ the contemplative mind.

It is time we put the mind in the heart through spiritual practice, thus waking up the contemplative mind. In so doing, we are able to perceive the reality of wholeness and the unity of existence, which will lead to taking greater responsibility for one another and our planet.

Secular society recognizes the value of contemplative practice. The masses are trending toward mindfulness. It's time more Christians get it too. The wisdom of conscious awareness is in the Christian lineage. God knows we've never needed to integrate it into the faith more than we need to today.

The Christian mystics mentioned in this book may have been ignorant of the information age we're living in, yet they identified our struggle—that we are fragmented and alienated from our Source and one another. These masters, and their powerful practices, can guide us toward reunion with love's ultimate ground, which opens us to personal and collective healing like nothing else can.

> NURTURING THE CONTEMPLATIVE MIND THROUGH SPIRITUAL PRACTICE HELPS CREATE BETTER CHRISTIANS, BETTER HUMANS.

Suffice it to say that we need to nurture the contemplative mind or "heart mind" that opens us to the mysterious and miraculous. Rational spirituality has gotten us only so far in relationship with God, one another, and the world. Bridging the rational with the contemplative will bring wholeness. Nurturing the contemplative mind through spiritual practice helps create better Christians, better humans. Activating unitive consciousness helps us co-create with God and mend our world.

No matter your profession or circumstances, it's time to wake up. Like Adrian at the Deepening Retreat, I hope you'll conjure up the courage to face whatever it is you're afraid of that keeps you from being alone, quiet, and still. It's time to bravely face reality.

UNCOVER YOUR ESSENCE

All those years ago in Freetown, Sierra Leone, I met a young woman who forever changed my life. Ravaged by war, Zoe had lost everything—her family, her home, and her education. Sitting in the wreckage, she boldly faced her pain and through her suffering uncovered

the depths of her essence. There she uprooted anger, hate, and ven-
geance and found the seedlings of forgiveness, love, and redemption.
Her tears watered those seeds, and in time she let go of blame and
uncovered compassion for the people of her country, all of whom had
been victimized in one way or another—even the perpetrators of
unspeakable violence.

I am forever indebted to Zoe and the people of Freetown. Men,
women, and children determined to be free from civil war unlocked
the door to freedom for me. Those brave survivors became my
liberators—both the girls who courageously shared the agony of their
victimization and the boys who humbly shared the torment of
their offenses. Their unabashed boldness in facing their reality shat-
tered the mold of my personality with its illusions and limitations.
There, in a land broken open by a war for blood diamonds, those
vulnerable women became midwives to my contemplative awakening.
Those tender boys unearthed my inner diamond.

You are stronger and more resilient than you realize. You can handle
the pain that hides inside and secretly influences everything, draining
the life out of you and those around you. In fact, with contemplative
practice, you can learn how to hold that pain and let it instruct you
and ultimately transform you.

Your family and community need you to be a courageous pilgrim
on the spiritual journey. God knows our world needs your bravery too.
The more of us who commit to the contemplative path—the path of
seeing, observing, and taking responsibility for our life through meditative practice—the more possible it will be to experience God's presence in the center of our being. From that center, we can build the
world we all want to live in.

Practice: Be and Do

Everything you need to live into your divine nature is within reach. You merely need to wake from your slumber, notice how you run and hide, and begin to take responsibility for your life by adopting a regular contemplative practice.

So, before you close these pages and move on to the next important endeavor, choose a spiritual practice and commit anew to staying awake. In addition to the contemplative prayer practices mentioned in these pages, consider the following simple exercises to help you stay awake when life threatens to lull you to sleep.

- Make a practice of turning off podcasts and music when you are driving. Listen to the silence.
- Choose one day a week to unplug from all digital devices. Practice this simple form of solitude and being present.
- Make regular time to get out in nature. After a walk or bike ride, sit on a park bench and soak in the sights, sounds, and smells. Sink into stillness.
- Adopt a puppy from a local rescue. That little creature will teach you everything you need know about contemplation and ultimate reality.

AFTERWORD

Kirsten Powers

MY JOURNEY INTO contemplative Christianity came at a crisis point as it does for so many. I had reached a place where I felt homeless in the church. My faith had become more of a stress than a balm in my life. I began to wonder: Am I even a Christian?

While I felt deeply connected to Jesus, I was increasingly alienated by the way so many churches presented his teachings and by how so many Christians, especially in public life, behaved. I started to wonder if perhaps I had misunderstood Jesus and that following him was not about loving other people, humility, sacrifice, and kindness but in fact about holding the "correct" theology or being the fiercest combatant in the American culture wars.

I had recently converted to Catholicism, where I felt more theologically and culturally at home. I naively expected it would also provide some sort of safe haven from the endless fighting among Christians over which political positions you needed to take in order to be considered a faithful believer. I loved that the Catholic Church was a global church, with views that didn't line up neatly with either political party in the United States. Instead, I discovered almost immediately the different Catholic factions at war with each other about, well, everything. Peace was elusive.

Added to this was the fact that I work in the increasingly toxic world of political journalism, which now had a new element: the election of a very controversial figure, which created more division in America than I had ever witnessed, or frankly thought was possible.

Amidst all this chaos, my prayer life ebbed and flowed, and I discovered that if I was able to remove myself from the daily stresses of life and focus only on God I would feel connected and calm. But once I set foot back into the "real world," I would find it difficult to maintain the kind of equilibrium and prayer life I sought and needed. Unless I was going to lock myself away from the world, something had to change.

After watching my increasing struggle with my faith, a friend recommended I go see Phileena and her husband, Chris, at the Gravity Center. I arrived confused and despondent and left a few days later filled with hope. I'll be forever grateful to both of them not just for putting the train back on the tracks, but for fundamentally transforming the way that I connect with God.

As Phileena does in this important book, she introduced me to the contemplative tradition, which goes back to the earliest days of Christianity. While most people associate contemplation only with Buddhism, in fact it is core to the Christian faith. But you don't need to be a Christian, or a believer of any kind, to benefit from this teaching. Contemplative spirituality is for everyone. It's an antidote to the hectic, materialistic, narcissistic world we live in. It's a way to help us "unlearn" all the lies we have been taught about what makes us worthy or valuable—our "programs for happiness" that never seem to deliver—and find true peace and meaning in our lives.

Critically, the contemplative tradition helps us also understand that we can't transform the world until we have our own inner transformation. It teaches us to move out of living from our ego, or "false self," and to connect to our "true self," which is who we really are and have always been. Once you begin bringing this kind of healing to yourself, you can bring healing to the world.

More than ever, we need this now. The world feels increasingly difficult to handle each day for so many. Yet, as Phileena instructs us, the solution isn't to check out. It's to become "contemplatives in action."

You are blessed to have discovered the perfect guide. Phileena is wise and learned, humble and kind, self-aware but gentle with herself, and emanates a depth and peace we should all long to have. She has come by it honestly through suffering and doubt and struggling through the dark and pain not knowing what she would find on the other side. She is brave and a truth seeker. We are all the beneficiaries of Phileena's journey. With her, you are in the best of hands.

I'm honored to have Phileena as a teacher, and thrilled you discovered this book. If you apply the practices she teaches, you will learn how to stay engaged and involved in changing the world without descending into despondency or burning out. The contemplative tradition truly is a game changer. Once you start practicing, you will be shocked by how something so simple can have such a profound effect on your life.

I hope, like me, you'll take the plunge into sacred solitude, silence, and stillness and there discover the most meaningful life you can live. Enjoy the journey!

ACKNOWLEDGMENTS

THE WORLD IS MADE BETTER by altruistic people who genuinely care for others and go out of their way to express their support. I have been fortunate to receive such love from a number of people who helped make this book possible.

First, to Chris, my life partner, who believes in me more than anyone I know. Thank you for giving of your precious time to take an interest in this work. The hours you devoted to reading and editing were truly sacrificial. Your reassurance for what I was able to communicate fueled me to keep going and helped me find internal resources that I didn't know were there. And your creative suggestions made this a far better book than it would have been. After all these years, you continue to teach me, lead me, and inspire me. I love you and am so grateful for you.

To Father Thomas Keating. All those years ago your teaching saved my life. Your presence has given me courage to die and find the life I've longed for. Thank you for your steadfastness.

To Father Richard Rohr. I cannot thank you enough for the generosity of your time, presence, and guidance over the years. You are the most fecund person I know. Your wisdom has been a beacon through the darkest hours of my spiritual journey. During some of the most turbulent of times, your heartfelt compassion was a balm for my soul. Thank you for being you and inviting us all into the divine dance.

To Debbie Sheehan. Your spiritual direction is such a refuge for me. Thank you for seeing me, hearing me, believing in me, and helping me find my way. You are such a grace to me.

To my friends who went out of their way to read the early drafts of this manuscript. Stuart Higginbotham, your wholehearted encouragement helped me remember the value of this book when the work seemed daunting. Your keen insights and input refined important facets of the otherwise nuanced aspects of contemplative spirituality. Mark Longhurst, you totally nailed it by identifying the most effete of chapters in the early draft. Thank you so much for ascertaining the weak link and challenging its development. That chapter, and consequently the book, reached its potential because of you. Rob O'Callaghan, thank you for taking such precise care with every word, sentence, paragraph, and chapter. Your attention to detail and consistency made all the difference. Amos Smith, thank you for your generous attention to a frail composition. With the mind of a scholar and the heart of a pastor, you elevated what was possible with this work.

To my coworkers. Anahi Salazar Angulo, something about the way you would ask about my writing always made me feel like the book mattered, that even just being a woman writing on spirituality was important enough. Thank you for your loving support. Melanie Kim, thank you for helping me manage my schedule so that I could carve out chunks of time to give this work the attention it deserved. Betty McGuire, thank you so much for helping with the nitty-gritty, behind the scenes administration of the book's release. One of my greatest joys is getting to work with you. I'm very grateful for the way each of you cheered me on in your unique way. In each of you, I see the best of the divine feminine. You give me hope for a society marked with equality and mutuality. You make the world a better place just by being you.

To Kathy Mansfield. Your labyrinth image featured in chapter five is stunning. No other practice captures the movements of the spiritual journey quite like the labyrinth. Knowing how dear the labyrinth is to you, I'm honored you would contribute one of yours with me and this book and its readers. Thank you for sharing in the spirit of *Mindful Silence* in such a personal way.

To my team at InterVarsity Press. To Cindy Bunch, associate publisher and director of editorial. Thank you for valuing the contemplative path and recognizing the need for this book in the market. Your keen advice and sincere support made all the difference as we drafted the structure for what *Mindful Silence* has become. To Elissa Schauer, associate managing editor. Your kindness during the copyediting phase meant the world to me. For a very technical process, you managed to transmute incredible warmth and genuine support. Thank you. To Andrew Bronson, senior marketing manager. From the beginning you had a hand in *Mindful Silence* being made possible. Thank you for believing in me and my voice from the outset. Thank you also for your thoughtful attention to the best ways to present this book to readers. I'm thankful for your recommendation to work with Lori Neff, marketing manager. Lori, you get this. You grasp how crucial contemplative spirituality is and you understand the readers who are ready for this work. Thank you for putting your heart and soul into the marketing strategy. To Christina Gilliland, assistant marketing manager. Thank you for keeping the process moving forward and always communicating with grace and enthusiasm. To Krista Clayton, senior publicist. Thank you for your determination and commitment to find various outlets for presenting *Mindful Silence* to receptive audiences. I am grateful for your energy and thoughtfulness for this important aspect of the book's maturation. And to Alisse Wissman, publicity manager, and Deborah Gonzalez, social media marketing manager. Thank you for your tireless oversight and considerate attention to detail that likely often goes unnoticed. This book will reach the people who need it because of you.

And finally, to you, my people who read my work and come to my retreats and meet with me for spiritual direction. You manifested this book. You needed it and you asked me for it. Thank you for motivating me. And thank you for your dedication to the contemplative journey. Your spiritual practice, your exploration of the soul's depths, and your courage to come out from hiding make all the difference in the world.

NOTES

1 SLEEPWALKING

[1]Much of the content in this section first appeared in Phileena Heuertz, "As You Love Yourself: Where Contemplation and Action Meet," *The Table*, May 7, 2014, https://cct.biola.edu/as-you-love-yourself-contemplation -action. Used with permission.

[2]Richard Rohr, "The Scapegoat Mechanism," Center for Action and Contemplation, April 30, 2017, https://cac.org/the-scapegoat-mechanism -2017-04-30; Richard Rohr, "The Myth of Redemptive Violence," Center for Action and Contemplation, May 1, 2017, https://cac.org/myth -redemptive-violence-2017-05-01 (emphasis in original).

[3]See Phileena Heuertz, *Pilgrimage of a Soul: Contemplative Spirituality for the Active Life*, rev. ed. (Downers Grove, IL: InterVarsity Press, 2017).

[4]Henri Nouwen, "Being the Beloved," sermon, November 22, 2012, www .youtube.com/watch?v=v8U4V4aaNWk.

[5]Some of this content first appeared in *Pilgrimage of a Soul*, 47.

[6]Much of the content here first appeared at "Enneagram," Gravity, https:// gravitycenter.com/join/enneagram. Used with permission.

2 WITHDRAWING TO ENGAGE

[1]Thomas Merton, *Conjectures of a Guilty Bystander* (New York: Doubleday, 1966), 81.

[2]Karl Rahner, *Theological Investigations*, vol. 20, *Concern for the Church* (New York: Crossroad, 1981), 149.

[3]Thomas Aquinas, *Summa Theologica* 2.188.6.

[4]Rahner, *Concern for the Church*, 149.

[5]To learn more about the impact of contemplative prayer on my active life, read *Pilgrimage of a Soul: Contemplative Spirituality for the Active Life*, rev. ed. (Downers Grove, IL: InterVarsity Press, 2017).

[6]When teaching the Enneagram, Chris Heuertz often emphasizes this aspect of the spiritual journey. The Enneagram is incredibly helpful for learning how to self-observe so we can self-correct. See his book *The Sacred Enneagram: Finding Your Unique Path to Spiritual Growth* (Grand Rapids: Zondervan, 2017), 70.

[7]Paul Tillich, *Systematic Theology* (Chicago: University of Chicago Press, 1951, 1973), 1:155.

[8]Thomas Merton, *Thoughts in Solitude* (New York: Farrar, Straus & Giroux, 1956, 1958), 103.

[9]James Finley, *Intimacy: The Divine Ambush*, CD, MP3 download (Center for Action and Contemplation, 2013), disc 4.

[10]Thomas Merton, *No Man Is an Island* (New York: Doubleday Image, 1955), 65.

[11]John Dear, *Thomas Merton, Peacemaker: Meditations on Merton, Peacemaking, and the Spiritual Life* (Maryknoll, NY: Orbis, 2015), 17.

[12]Robert Anthony Cashen, *Solitude in the Thought of Thomas Merton* (Kalamazoo, MI: Cistercian, 1981), 315.

[13]Thomas Merton, *New Seeds of Contemplation* (New York: New Directions, 1949), 42.

[14]Cashen, *Solitude in the Thought of Thomas Merton*, 51.

[15]Merton, *Conjectures of a Guilty Bystander*, 140-42.

[16]Merton, *New Seeds of Contemplation*, 34.

[17]Cashen, *Solitude in the Thought of Thomas Merton*, 66.

[18]Merton, *New Seeds of Contemplation*, 34-35.

[19]Merton, *New Seeds of Contemplation*, 47.

[20]Thomas Merton, *The Inner Experience* (San Francisco: Harper, 2003), 16.

[21]Merton, *New Seeds of Contemplation*, 33.

[22]Richard Rohr, "Transforming Our Pain," Richard Rohr's Daily Meditations, February 26, 2016, https://cac.org/transforming-our-pain-2016-02-26.

[23]Pope John Paul II, "Orientale Lumen," Apostolic Letter, May 2, 1995, I:6, note 14; https://w2.vatican.va/content/john-paul-ii/en/apost_letters /1995/documents/hf_jp-ii_apl_19950502_orientale-lumen.html.

3 FINDING LIBERATION BY DISCERNMENT

[1]Janna Quitney Anderson and Lee Rainie, "Millennials Will Benefit *and* Suffer Due to Their Hyperconnected Lives," Pew Internet and American Life Project, February 29, 2012, www.pewinternet.org/files/old-media

//Files/Reports/2012/PIP_Future_of_Internet_2012_Young_brains _PDF.pdf.

[2]Henri Nouwen, *Making All Things New: An Invitation to the Spiritual Life* (New York: HarperOne, 1981), 67. For more information on the subject of obedience, see Phileena Heuertz, "From Absurdity to Obedience," *The Cry* 17, no. 2.6 (2011), http://wordmadeflesh.org/from-absurdity-to -obedience.

[3]George E. Ganss, SJ, *Ignatius of Loyola: The Spiritual Exercises and Selected Works* (New York: Paulist Press, 1991), rule 313.

[4]John Neafsey, *A Sacred Voice Calling: Personal Vocation and Social Conscience* (Maryknoll, NY: Orbis, 2006), 1.

[5]Enneagram enthusiasts will want to note that these are the three intelligent centers located in the Enneagram.

[6]Ganss, *Ignatius of Loyola*, rule 331.

[7]Ganss, *Ingatius of Loyola*, rule 330.

4 DISCOVERING DARKNESS IS LIGHT

[1]Richard Rohr, "The Mystery of Suffering," Richard Rohr's Daily Meditation, January 24, 2018, https://cac.org/the-mystery-of-suffering-2018-01-24/.

[2]Julian of Norwich, *Showings*, chap. 53, in *The Writings of Julian of Norwich: A Vision Showed to a Devout Woman and A Revelation of Love*, ed. Nicholas Watson and Jacqueline Jenkins (State College: Pennsylvania State University Press, 2006), 295. (Sentences presented here are adapted from Julian's Middle English.)

[3]Julian of Norwich, *Showings*, chap. 9, in Watson and Jenkins, *Writings*, 155.

[4]Julian of Norwich, *Showings*, chap. 51, in Watson and Jenkins, *Writings*, 279.

[5]Julian of Norwich, *Showings*, chap. 65, in Watson and Jenkins, *Writings*, 329.

[6]Julian of Norwich, *Showings*, chap. 51, in Watson and Jenkins, *Writings*, 279.

[7]John of the Cross, *Dark Night of the Soul: A Masterpiece in the Literature of Mysticism*, ed. E. Allison Peers (New York: Doubleday, 1959), 37.

[8]John of the Cross, *The Ascent of Mount Carmel*, book 2, chap. 22, in Kieran Kavanaugh, *John of the Cross: Selected Writings* (New York: Paulist Press, 1987), 127-35.

[9]John of the Cross, *Ascent of Mount Carmel*, book 1, chap. 13, and *The Dark Night*, book 1, chap. 9, in Kavanaugh, *John of the Cross*, 76-79, 180-84.

[10]John of the Cross, *Ascent of Mount Carmel*, book 3, chap. 6, in Kavanaugh, *John of the Cross*, 147.

[11]John of the Cross, *Ascent of Mount Carmel*, book 2, chap. 26, in Kavanaugh, *John of the Cross*, 139.

[12]Richard Hauser, *Moving in the Spirit: Becoming a Contemplative in Action* (Mahwah, NJ: Paulist Press, 1986), 13.

[13]John of the Cross, *Ascent of Mount Carmel*, book 2, chap. 17, in Kavanaugh, *John of the Cross*, 123.

[14]John of the Cross, *The Living Flame of Love*, stanza 1, par. 13, in Kavanaugh, *John of the Cross*, 298.

[15]Kieran Kavanaugh, introduction to *The Dark Night*, in *John of the Cross*, 158.

[16]John of the Cross, *Dark Night*, book 2, chap. 11, in Kavanaugh, *John of the Cross*, 208.

[17]John of the Cross, *Dark Night*, book 1, in Kavanaugh, *John of the Cross*, 162-97.

[18]John of the Cross, *Living Flame*, stanza 1, par. 13, in Kavanaugh, *John of the Cross*, 298.

[19]John of the Cross, *Dark Night*, book 1, chap. 12, in Kavanaugh, *John of the Cross*, 193.

[20]John of the Cross, *Living Flame*, stanza 2, in Kavanaugh, *John of the Cross*, 303.

[21]John of the Cross, *Ascent of Mount Carmel*, book 3, chap. 16, and *Living Flame*, in Kavanaugh, *John of the Cross*, 150, 293-94.

[22]John of the Cross, *The Spiritual Canticle*, stanza 28, in Kavanaugh, *John of the Cross*, 266-69.

[23]John of the Cross, *Spiritual Canticle*, stanza 28, par. 10, in Kavanaugh, *John of the Cross*, 269.

5 EXPLORING A DEEP WELL

[1]I first heard this quote paraphrased by Dr. Sam Kamaleson of World Vision. Its origin is disputed.

[2]I was first introduced to this psycho-spiritual categorization by Ken Wilber and Richard Rohr at the Center for Action and Contemplation's 2017 Conspire conference in Albuquerque, New Mexico. "Growing up," "waking up," and "cleaning up" are helpful categories for understanding the transformational process of being human.

[3]Richard Rohr offers the helpful language of "container" in his teaching on identity and transformation.

[4]Mary Oliver, "The Summer Day," in *Devotions: The Selected Poems of Mary Oliver* (New York: Penguin Press, 2017).

6 DYING FOR LIFE

[1]For more information on this historic gathering see Phileena Heuertz, "New Contemplative Leaders Exchange," Gravity, https://gravitycenter .com/new-contemplative-leaders-exchange.

[2]Drew Jackson, "The Contemplative Way as a Practice in Death," Gravity blog, December 1, 2016, https://gravitycenter.com/life-found-dying.

[3]Joydeep Thakur, "Kolkata Fourth Most Polluted Megacity with Coarse Dust in the Air," *Hindustan Times*, October 1, 2016, www.hindustantimes.com /kolkata/kolkata-fourth-most-polluted-megacity-with-coarse-dust -particles-in-the-air/story-0YG5764omV8FrH400cLJ7N.html.

[4]Suman Chakrabortil, "Air Pollution Level in Kolkata Among Country's Highest," *Times of India*, January 3, 2017, http://timesofindia.indiatimes .com/city/kolkata/air-pollution-level-in-kolkata-among-countrys-highest /articleshow/56310086.cms.

[5]Subhro Niyogil, "Kolkata's Poor Poorer Than the Rest," *Times of India*, September 12, 2012, http://timesofindia.indiatimes.com/city/kolkata /Kolkatas-poor-poorer-than-the-rest/articleshow/16367595.cms.

[6]Quoted in Shira Atkins, "Seane Corn on Personal Transformation and Social Justice," Sonima, May 1, 2015, www.sonima.com/meditation /seane-corn.

[7]Brian Kolodiejchuk, *Mother Teresa: Come Be My Light: The Private Writings of the Saint of Calcutta* (New York: Doubleday, 2007), 1.

7 UNKNOWING TO KNOW

[1]Richard Rohr uses the terminology order, disorder, reorder. See "Order, Disorder, Reorder," Richard Rohr Daily Meditations, February 23, 2016, https://cac.org/order-disorder-reorder-2016-02-23. Walter Brueggemann uses the terminology orientation, disorientation, reorientation. See his book *Spirituality of the Psalms* (Minneapolis: Fortress Press, 2002).

[2]William Johnston, *The Cloud of Unknowing and The Book of Privy Counseling* (New York: Doubleday, 1973), 10.

[3]Richard Rohr, "The Mystery of Suffering," Richard Rohr's Daily Meditation, January 24, 2018, https://cac.org/the-mystery-of-suffering-2018-01-24/.

[4]Richard Rohr, "Cross as Agenda," Richard Rohr's Daily Meditation, May 5, 2017, https://cac.org/cross-as-agenda-2017-05-05.

[5]Johnston, *Cloud of Unknowing*, 53-54.

8 WAKING UP

[1]Adrian Blake, "In the Recording Studio of Life, God Is the Room Tone," personal blog, April 7, 2014, www.adrianblake.me/personal/in-the-recording-studio-of-life-god-is-the-room-tone.

gravity

a center for contemplative activism

The spiritual journey makes life worth living, yet at times it can be really difficult to navigate on our own. Phileena meets monthly with her spiritual director as a way of staying rooted in the journey and connected to the Divine. Phileena also provides spiritual direction for others. Certified by the Jesuits in the contemplative-evocative method of spiritual direction, Phileena is an internationally recognized spiritual director meeting with people from all walks of life in person or over the phone or Skype. To learn more about spiritual direction or to inquire about meeting with Phileena visit gravitycenter.com/join/spiritual-direction/.

formatio

TRADITION. EXPERIENCE.
TRANSFORMATION.

Formatio books from InterVarsity Press follow the rich tradition of the church in the journey of spiritual formation. These books are not merely about being informed, but about being transformed by Christ and conformed to his image. Formatio stands in InterVarsity Press's evangelical publishing tradition by integrating God's Word with spiritual practice and by prompting readers to move from inward change to outward witness. InterVarsity Press uses the chambered nautilus for Formatio, a symbol of spiritual formation because of its continual spiral journey outward as it moves from its center. We believe that each of us is made with a deep desire to be in God's presence. Formatio books help us to fulfill our deepest desires and to become our true selves in light of God's grace.